KENTUCKY
LEGENDS & LORE

KENTUCKY
LEGENDS & LORE

ALAN BROWN

THE
History
PRESS

Published by The History Press
Charleston, SC
www.historypress.com

Front cover, top left: courtesy of Wikimedia Commons; *top center*: courtesy of the author; *top right*: courtesy of the author; *bottom*: Wikimedia Commons.
Back cover: Wikimedia Commons; *inset*: courtesy of Wikimedia Commons.

Unless otherwise noted, all images are courtesy of the author.

First published 2021

ISBN 9781467149822

Library of Congress Control Number: 2021943807

Notice: The information in this book is true and complete to the best of our knowledge. It is offered without guarantee on the part of the author or The History Press. The author and The History Press disclaim all liability in connection with the use of this book.

To Marilyn

CONTENTS

Introduction   9

1. Civil War Legends   11
2. Legendary Bad Men   29
3. Legendary Cemeteries   41
4. Legendary Characters   53
5. Legendary Locations   65
6. Legendary Lost Treasure   109
7. Mysteries from the Skies   115
8. Mysterious Deaths   127
9. Mysterious Monsters   135
10. Native American Legends   147
11. University Legends   153

Works Cited   165
About the Author   176

INTRODUCTION

Kentucky is not a typical southern state. It located in the Upland South, bordered on the north by Illinois, Indiana and Ohio. During the Civil War, it was a border state, even though sixty-eight counties passed an Ordinance of Secession on November 20, 1861. Despite Kentucky's neutral status, it was represented by the center star on the Confederate battle flag. Although agriculture is an important part of Kentucky's economy, its primary cash crop is tobacco, not cotton. Kentucky also produces 95 percent of the world's bourbon and is known as a center of horse breeding, owing in large part to the soil's high calcium content. In the minds of many Americans, Kentucky is the "Bluegrass State." Other people think of it as the "Dark and Bloody Ground," an allusion to its violent past. In many ways, Kentucky's folklore is as distinctive as the other aspects of the state.

Even though many fewer battles were fought in Kentucky than in other Southern states, its folklore boasts a number of impressive Civil War legends. As with other states of the Confederacy, many of Kentucky's antebellum homes were enlisted into service as field hospitals, like Maple Hill Manor in Springfield. As one might expect, the spirits of some of the men who died in Maple Hill Manor are still there. The spirits of some of the more than seven thousand men who perished at Perryville National Battlefield are still on duty—so is the ghost of one of the horses.

Kentucky's legends concern some men and women who were very good and some who were very bad. The most legendary—and iconic—frontiersman in the state was Daniel Boone, who achieved fame as the trailblazer through the Cumberland Gap. Edgar Cayce devoted his psychic skills to healing people.

Among the bad men, the Harp brothers—America's first serial killers—are undoubtedly the worst. Rod Ferrell, the "Vampire Cult Killer," and Donald Harvey, the "Angel of Death," run a close second and third. Even Jesse James made a stop in Kentucky.

Visitors to Kentucky have a large number of haunted places to choose from. Some of these sites are cemeteries, such as Cave Hill Cemetery in Louisville. A few of these burial grounds are famous because they have just one occupant, such as the grave in Harrodsburg Spring Park. Among the weird and bizarre sites in Kentucky are the Witches' Tree in Old Louisville; the Jailer's Inn in Bardstown; Mammoth Cave in Edmonson, Hart and Barren Counties; the Sand Mountain Lights in Jefferson and Means Counties; and the Seelbach Hotel in Louisville.

Treasure hunters will be intrigued by the legends of lost caches of gold and silver. Tales include the Sprinkle Dollars in Lewis County, Doc Brown's outlaw gold in Grayson County and Jonathan Swift's lost silver mine somewhere in eastern Kentucky. Finding buried treasure would be wonderful, but reading about it is almost as much fun.

Even though Kentucky is in the middle of a list ranking states by UFO sightings, it has some of the most high-profile occurrences. The most bizarre UFO encounter is undoubtedly the goblin attack on a family farm in Hopkinsville in 1955. Some UFO encounters were too close for comfort, such as Captain Thomas Mantell's plane crash, the coal train collision in Paintsville and the Stanford alien abduction.

All states have tales about strange or mysterious deaths, and Kentucky is no exception. Some of these stories focus on the lengthy process of determining the identity of the deceased, such as Tent Girl in Lexington and Mountain Jane Doe in Harlan County. A couple of these tales are memorable because of the bizarre manner in which the person died, like Olivia Hatcher's death in Pikesville and the face in the cupola window in Russellville.

Legends about monsters lurking in the hills and forests of Kentucky have been told ever since settlers came into the region. Fishermen still spin yarns about the Lake Harrington Monster in Mercer, Garrard and Boyle Counties. Young people still flock to the Pole Lick Trestle in Louisville in the hope of catching sight of the Goat Man. Kentucky's version of Big Foot—the Hillbilly Beast—has been terrorizing residents and hunters for many years.

There is no substitute for visiting a beautiful, storied state like Kentucky. The next best way to sample the "Kentucky experience" is by reading about it. So sit back, pour yourself a glass of bourbon (if you are so inclined and old enough) and enjoy reading about Kentucky's legends and lore.

Chapter 1

CIVIL WAR LEGENDS

MAPLE HILL MANOR (SPRINGFIELD)

Forty-one-year-old Thomas McElroy built his Greek Revival planation home on 949 acres between 1848 and 1851. He presented it to his twenty-one-year-old bride, Sarah Jane Maxwell, as a wedding present. Of their seven children, four died between the ages of one and two. Sarah followed her children in death when she was forty-eight years old; her husband passed away at the age of sixty. Death on a much larger scale visited Maple Hill Manor during the Battle of Perryville on October 8, 1862. Approximately 75,000 soldiers fought in what became Kentucky's largest Civil War battle. At day's end, more than 7,600 men were listed as wounded, killed or missing in action. Because of its proximity to the battlefield, Maple Hill Manor was one of several plantation homes in the region that served as a field hospital for General Braxton Bragg's 2,635 wounded men. After the war, the mansion became a popular dinner hall and the Foster Children's Home, where over 300 foster children received care. The home is also known as the birthplace of New York Giants quarterback Phil Simms. He achieved fame as the MVP of Super Bowl XXI. In 1987, Bob and Kay Carroll converted the antebellum home into a bed-and-breakfast. In the early 2000s, they sold the business to Todd Allen and Tyler Horton. Their 15-acre farm includes horses, alpacas, llamas, cats, dogs and, some say, a host of ghosts.

Maple Hill Manor was built between 1848 and 1851. Following the Battle of Perryvile, the mansion served as a field hospital.

Ghostly activity has been reported throughout Maple Hill Manor. In 1999, Bob and Kay Carroll told author William Lynwood Montell that, one summer night, two couples were staying in rooms on the second floor. After they went to dinner, Bob and Kay's family sat down for dinner. Suddenly, Bob heard footsteps moving back and forth on the second floor for two to three minutes. Thinking that one of the guests had returned, Bob looked out the front door, but no one was there. Bob walked over to the bottom of the stairs and said, in a loud voice, "Can I help you?" When he received no response, Bob, his son and their dog went to the upstairs rooms, but no one was there. He believed that "some of those Confederate soldiers are still with us."

In July 1999, Kay was fixing some of the lamps near the front door when she heard someone knock with one of the old-fashioned knockers. No one was there when she opened the door. At the same time, she felt a cool breeze pass by, causing goose bumps to rise on her arms. This was the only time she had this experience.

The Carrolls had other weird disruptions to their everyday routine. They occasionally detected the strong fragrance of perfume or flowers in certain rooms. In one of the photos they received from a guest, a streak of light can clearly be seen floating into the bedroom. A little boy was trying to ride down the bannister on the second floor when he fell off and was killed. The ghost of the little boy may be responsible for turning lights off and on in the Stephen Foster Room. He has been sighted watching guests while they slept. In the Lincoln Library, a chair turns itself toward a window, some say, so that an invisible presence can have a better view of the farm. One night, a couple staying in the Honeymoon Room were reading in bed when, suddenly, all of the lights went off. In 2008, a guest sleeping in the Kentucky Artisans Room heard the sound of someone breathing heavily in the middle of the night. He was all alone at the time. In 2021, a woman and her daughter were staying in the second-floor Clara Barton Room, which adjoins the Harriett Beecher Stowe Room, where surgeries were performed during the Civil War. During the night, the woman heard the security chain rattling on the door. Later, they head the sounds of a woman crying and a man groaning in the room next door.

The Harriet Beecher Stowe Room is very active, probably because eighteen cots were set up here to accommodate wounded soldiers who were brought for medical care following the Battle of Perryville. The story goes that the floor was painted blue to cover up the bloodstains. The rocking chair that was placed on the carpeting over the bloodstains has rocked by itself at times. Female guests have felt someone scratching or cutting on their arms inside the room between 2:00 a.m. and 3:00 a.m. Invisible hands are said to have pulled the covers up to the necks of sleeping guests and down to their feet. Guests have seen a male apparition standing in the closet and lying on the four-poster bed. Todd was changing sheets in the room one morning when he saw the ghost of the Black nanny, Mammy Anne, sitting in the chair by the bed, staring into the closet. "When she turned her head to look at me, she zipped up in the ceiling," Todd said. "It looked like she had been sucked up in a giant vacuum cleaner." One of the guests believed that Mammy Anne is a protective spirit who has a strong attachment to the room that once served as the nursery.

In 2017, a woman was staying in the Jefferson Davis Room with her husband following the reenactment of the Battle of Perryville. In the middle of the night, she was awakened by the uncomfortable feeling that someone had touched her. Her husband was sound asleep at the time. She drifted off to sleep and was awakened once again, this time by the sound of the fire alarm. When she turned on the light, the alarm turned off. She turned off the light and went back to sleep. A few minutes later, the alarm turned on

The floor underneath the rug in the Harriet Beecher Stowe Room was painted blue to cover up bloodstains from surgeries performed there. The rocking chair is said to rock on its own.

once again and stopped beeping when she turned on the light. Following a few more repetitions of the fire alarm going on and off, the couple packed up and left at 4:00 a.m. The next morning, the woman contacted her sister, who was sleeping with her husband in the room just below hers. She reported hearing nothing out of the ordinary during the night.

Tina Standiford, the manager of Maple Hill Manor, said that another problem with a fire alarm was reported by guests staying in the Lincoln Library Room. Tina received a phone call from the guests around midnight, complaining that the fire alarm in their room would not stop buzzing. When Tina walked into the room a few minutes later, she noticed that the fire alarm box was hanging about twelve feet from the floor. "I didn't want to go to the barn and get the fourteen-foot ladder," Tina said, "so I yelled at the ghost to stop messing with the fire alarm." The guests had no more complaints for the rest of the night.

Tina said that another paranormal event took place in the Lincoln Room in 2019, when a military man and his wife booked the Lincoln Library Room for the night. While he was bringing in their luggage, he noticed the

The fire alarm in the Lincoln Room turned on by itself. The manager made it stop by ordering the ghost to "stop messing around!"

television. "My wife and I watch T.V. once in a while," he said, "but we don't watch the news as a rule because it is too depressing." The next morning over breakfast, Tina asked the gentleman how he spent the night. He replied, "We slept just fine until the television came on by itself. And guess what the program was—it was the news!"

On June 12, 2021, my wife and I celebrated our forty-fifth wedding anniversary at Maple Hill Manor with her two brothers and sister and their spouses, as well as her nephew and our daughter and her husband. The next morning, my sister-in-law Julia Wolfe told Tina Standiford over breakfast that she was awakened during the night by a thumping sound a few feet from her room on the first floor. My other sister-in-law, Laurie Quick, corroborated Julia's account, stating that she also heard the sound at midnight. Smiling, Tina said that many guests on the first floor have heard that sound. She told them that Thomas and Sarah McElroy's five-year-old son had climbed up on the banister on the second floor just a few days before a section of the banister broke off, and he fell to his death. His residual spirit is still reenacting his tragic death.

A section of the bannister was replaced after a little boy fell off the stairway.

After Tina finished her story, Julia said that that was not the only weird thing that happened in the Stephen Foster Room the night before. Around midnight, Julia dreamed of being chased outside by a little girl with pigtails. The girl was wearing a long dress. Nodding her head, Tina replied that she knew who that ghost was, too. A couple of years earlier, Tina and her daughter were cleaning the Harriet Beecher Stowe Room. Suddenly, her daughter exclaimed that there was a little girl with pigtails standing in the doorway. She was visible for just a few seconds. Tina went back to her cleaning, but the bottle of disinfectant she was using was gone. She and her daughter looked everywhere in the room but were unable to find it. About an hour later, the pair moved over to the Jefferson Davis Room. They had not been cleaning for very long before Tina found the disinfectant hidden behind one of the curtains. She does not know the identity of the child. All she knows about her is that she likes to play jokes on people.

My wife, Marilyn, and I have also had uncanny experiences inside Maple Hill Manor. We were attracted to the bed-and-breakfast by the reports of guests hearing disembodied footsteps and knocking sounds at night. One guest even claimed to have had strange dreams while seeping in one of the rooms. Marilyn and I fully expected to have some sort of paranormal experience that night, and we were not disappointed. We were sleeping in the Elizabeth Maddox Roberts Room when she was awakened by two thumping sounds outside the door around 3:00 a.m. She also felt as if someone was poking her in the side. We both agreed that someone—or something—was trying to get her attention that night.

As my wife and I were checking out of Maple Hill Manor, Tina Standiford told us that she has been frightened only a couple of times inside the house. The thumping sound on the first floor by the staircase always sends chills up her spine. She was unnerved on another occasion by the sound of women talking on the second floor after the last guest had left. For the most part, though, Tina feels very comfortable inside the house. Her suspicions that the spirit of Sarah McElroy likes her were confirmed by a ghost-hunting group and a medium who sensed that the "lady of the house" was very fond of Tina. Tina added that she is fond of Sarah as well.

PERRYVILLE BATTLEFIELD STATE HISTORIC SITE (PERRYVILLE)

By 1862, the Union army was bent on taking Kentucky for President Abraham Lincoln, who said, "I hope to have God on my side, but I must have Kentucky. I think to lose Kentucky is nearly the same as to lose the whole game." In the summer of 1862, Union general Don Carlos Buell was converging on Chattanooga. To relieve the pressure on Chattanooga, Bragg moved his vastly outnumbered forces to Kentucky, hoping that enlistments would swell his ranks. The number of recruits who joined Bragg's army fell far below his expectations. By October, Buell was headed for Perryville while Bragg pushed on to Frankfort. On October 8, Buell's scouts were fired upon along Peter's Hill while searching for water. The fighting escalated as General Philip Sheridan moved his army up the road. When the fighting ended the next morning, Buell was totally unaware that a battle had taken place, as he could not hear the fighting from his headquarters at the Dorsey House. By 10:00 a.m., General Leonidas Polk's troops had arrived at Perryville. Bragg chose the Crawford House as his headquarters. At 2:00 p.m., Confederate forces waged a direct attack on Union general Alexander McCook's troops at Walker's Bend, forcing him to withdraw. Around the same time, Polk was almost captured by Union troops from Indiana whom he mistook for

Confederate soldiers. Doctor's Creek was the site of some of the bloodiest fighting. Colonel George P. Webster's brigade pushed the Confederates back to the Russell House on the Mackville Road. Brigadier General Patrick R. Cleburne continued directing his Confederate forces, despite the fact that he had been wounded. Because Sheridan was ordered not to engage the Confederates, he watched helplessly as McCook's army was battered by the enemy. At 4:00 p.m., his commanding officer, General Buell, was dining at his headquarters, still oblivious to the fact that a battle was going on. At 4:15 p.m., Confederate colonel Samuel Powell attempted, unsuccessfully, to repulse Sheridan's division. Realizing that he was too outnumbered to continue, Bragg moved into eastern Tennessee, ending the Confederate sweep into Kentucky. By battle's end, 3,145 Confederates lay dead on the battlefield; Buell lost 3,696 men. Federals collected their fallen comrades and moved them to regimental graves in a cemetery along the Springfield Pike for a proper burial. Confederate casualties were left on the battlefield for three days before finally being moved to the Bottom family's farm. The Confederates' push into Kentucky had come to a blood-soaked conclusion.

The carnage left in the aftermath of the bloodiest battle in Kentucky's history made an indelible psychic impression on the landscape. Consequently, Perryville Battlefield Park has become popular with paranormal researchers. The park even offers a ghost seminar and a ghost hunt for visitors three times a year. Joan House, the program coordinator and preservation specialist of the Perryville Battlefield State Historic Site, told writer Patti Star that the most commonly sighted spirit is the ghost of Patrick Cleburne's horse, which was shot out from under him when he was charging the Union lines. "Soon after the battle, the locals would report hearing a horse galloping by or near them," House said, "but when they would look for the horse, there was never one around." House added that one night, when she was camping with a group of reenactors, they all heard the pounding of a horse's hooves on the pavement. "We thought that maybe one of the horses in the camp had gotten loose," House said, "so we set out to find it." After searching the area with their flashlights, they counted the horses and discovered that none of them were missing. At that moment, she realized that they had had an encounter with Patrick Cleburne's horse.

On another occasion, two historians who were camping with a group of reenactors were sleeping in their tent when a man, dressed like a soldier, lifted their tent flap and asked them if they had seen one of his men. One of the historians asked the soldier who he was, and he gave his name and rank. He then yelled the man's name several times before leaving and walking over

The ghost of Patrick Cleburne's horse is the most frequently sighted apparition at the Perryville National Battlefield.

to the neighboring tent. They followed him to the tent, but he was nowhere to be found. Afterward, the historians conducted a search in the records and found the names of both men in the list of soldiers killed during the battle.

Squire Henry Bottom's house is another haunted site on the battlefield. In the heat of the battle, hand-to-hand fighting took place on Bottom's property, not far from his house. For several months after the battle, the Bottom House was used as a field hospital. Bottom and one of his slaves buried the bodies of Confederate soldiers who had been left behind by General Braxton Bragg in his rush to evade the oncoming Union forces. In 1996, the Perryville Enhancement Project undertook the task of restoring the Bottom House to its 1870 appearance. During the renovation, a couple of workers were walking through the attic when they found a bloodstained door that had probably been used as a makeshift operating table. A few years later, several Civil War reenactors who spent the night in the Bottom House experienced firsthand the psychic residue of battle that permeates the house. In the book *Haunted Battlefields of the South*, authors Bryan Bush and Thomas Freese recounted the men's otherworldly encounters. One of the reenactors

The spirits of some of the soldiers killed on the property are said to haunt the Bottom House.

entered the house and was overcome by nausea. After stepping outside and regaining his composure, he told his friend that he was sickened by the acrid smell of blood. Another reenactor was walking down the stairs when he felt something push him from behind. The Bottom House's legacy of violence and death is truly a tangible thing.

Interestingly enough, a feature of the battlefield's landscape is said to be haunted as well. In his book *Devil's Hollow and Other Kentucky Ghost Stories*, author Michael Paul Henson said that in 1972, he decided to visit Perryville National Battlefield at night. He parked his car on the roadside and began walking down the old wagon road toward Doctor's Creek. Suddenly, the gentle buzzing of insects was disrupted by the thunderous stomping of hundreds of feet running through the leaves. He heard the heavy panting of many exhausted men. After a few minutes, the strange sounds faded away. A few days later, Henson examined firsthand accounts of the battle and learned that a relief column of several companies of Confederate soldiers had hurried down the old wagon road to assist their comrades ninety years before his strange experience at Doctor's Creek.

Author Michael Henson heard the residual sounds of ghostly soldiers and wagons splashing across Doctor's Creek.

The ineradicable bloodstains on the floor of the Dye House bear mute witness to the surgeries performed there during the Battle of Perryville.

Jennifer Kirkland, a member of Spirit Hunters of Central Kentucky (SHOCK), has conducted several investigations at the battlefield. She says that one of the most haunted spots is the Dye House, which served as the headquarters of Confederate general Simon B. Buckner and as a field hospital. The bloodstains in the wood floor upstairs bear mute testament to the surgeries performed there. During electronic voice phenomenon (EVP) sessions, the group has received two different answers when it asked who the president of the United States was during the Civil War: Abraham Lincoln and Jefferson Davis.

Kirkland, who is also the preservation and program coordinator for the park, has experienced paranormal activity in her office as well. "I'm in my office and I hear people talking to me, and there's nobody else in this building," she said. Occasionally, the spirits announce their presence by playing with the exhibits. "There's no real explanation for why a mannequin's head has been pulled off and is now in the middle of the floor," she said.

THE LEGEND OF REBEL ROCK (PUTNEY)

Located between the towns of Cumberland and Harlan, the cliff that has come to be known as Rebel Rock overlooks the Old Laden Trail. During the Civil War, Rebel Rock was used as a hiding place and as a lookout point for soldiers passing through Harlan County, which, for the most part, sided with the Union. Resentment against the South escalated as Confederate troops began combing the countryside for food. One of these foraging raids earned the geological formation its name. The story goes that members of the local Home Guard, formed to protect farms and homesteads from marauding Confederates, caught sight of a group of soldiers searching for food. They chased one of the soldiers up a spur of Pine Mountain in the Poor Fork area. With no place to go, the Confederate soldier is said to have jumped off the cliff, either to escape or to commit suicide. In a variant of the legend, the man was thrown off the cliff by his pursuers. According to a newspaper account of the incident published in the *Harlan Daily Enterprise* in 1953, the soldier was one of three Confederates who were sneaking around Putnam in an attempt to steal food from the locals. They climbed up a rocky ridge to escape the crowd that was chasing them, but when faced with the prospect of falling or jumping off the cliff, "two of the men turned around and tried to shoot their way out of their hopeless situation. Both of them were killed by the outraged citizens of Poor Fork." The article ends with the fate of the last remaining rebel, who was standing alone "high up on the side of pine Mountain…[on] a huge rock, larger than a building.…As the angry citizens closed around the rock, the intruder fell from the rock to his death."

The identity of the rebel for whom the rock was named was unknown until the posting of an article by Andrew Smith on the website Medium on June 30, 2015. Smith wrote that the Confederate soldier was Captain Thomas Crupper, who enlisted in Company F of Brazelton's Third Tennessee Cavalry Battalion in 1861. He was captured by the Union army two years later and returned to Harlan County. In February 1864, Crupper and several other men from the county traveled to Camp Nelson to join the Union army. He deserted and returned to Harlan County to be with his wife, Ruth. One night, the Metcalf brothers—Ambrose, Adrian and James—caught Crupper trying to steal a ham from their smokehouse to feed the six men who were with him. The Confederates scattered. Crupper was trapped on the brink of the rocky spur at Pine Mountain. He tried to resist but was thrown off the cliff by the Metcalf brothers. They retrieved his body and tossed it in a crevice only one hundred yards from the Metcalf cemetery. By all accounts, Crupper's remains are still there. His only monument is the rocky cliff called Rebel Rock.

THE HUNT-MORGAN HOUSE (LEXINGTON)

During the Civil War, John Hunt Morgan's exploits as the leader of "Morgan's Raiders" earned him the nickname the "Thunderbolt of the Confederacy." Morgan is best known for his thousand-mile raid through Indiana and Ohio in 1863. After his capture and imprisonment, Morgan escaped from the Ohio State Penitentiary. He was shot and killed by a Union private in Greenville, Tennessee, on September 3, 1863. Hopemont was also home to John Wesley Hunt's great-grandson, Dr. Thomas Hunt Morgan, who was born there in 1866. Dr. Hunt went on to win the Nobel Prize for his work in physiology. In 1955, the Foundation for the Preservation of Historic Lexington and Fayette County saved Hopemont from demolition. The organization changed the name of the house to the Hunt-Morgan House and restored it to its nineteenth-century splendor. Today, the antebellum home is open to the public as a house museum. The building also houses the

The ghost of a motherly house slave named Mammy Bouviette appears on the third floor of the Hunt-Morgan House. *Courtesy of Wikimedia Commons.*

Alexander T. Hunt Civil War Museum. The collection includes many Civil War artifacts. The Hunt-Morgan House is also known for its legends.

The first of these stories dates back to the Civil War. In 1863, John Hunt Morgan returned to Lexington in the hope of receiving a kiss from his mother, Henrietta Hunt Morgan, who was living in Hopemont at the time. Despite the fact that the Union army had set up camp in Granz Park in front of Hopemont, Morgan rode his horse up the front steps and kissed his mother in the entry hall. He then galloped out the back door with Union soldiers hot on his tail.

The Hunt-Morgan House also has a ghost legend. Mammy Bouviette was a house slave who always wore the red shoes that John Hunt-Morgan had given her. Many people believe that her spirit remains in the Hunt-Morgan House because of her abiding love for the Hunt family. For generations, the ghost of Mammy Bouviette was believed to be present by the bedside of sick children. Even if the children died, their parents drew comfort from their belief that she would care for them in heaven. Her apparition has been sighted in the hallways and on the third floor of the Hunt-Morgan House.

The Octagon Hall (Franklin)

Andrew Jackson Caldwell began work on what was to become the most unique house in Simpson County in 1847. Work on Octagon Hall was finished in 1859. Each floor of the eight-sided, two-and-one-half story brick house has 876 square feet. Caldwell lived in the house with his wife, Lizzie, and their daughter Elizabeth. His slaves made all of the bricks onsite, including the five-sided corner bricks. They also cut and shaped the huge blocks of Bowling Green white limestone that were transported from a quarry. A Confederate sympathizer, Caldwell worked his cattle farm with twenty-five slaves. In the wake of the Confederate army's evacuation of Bowling Green, Union troops took over Caldwell's farm in February 1862, slaughtering his cattle and poisoning his water. After the Federals moved on, the Octagon Hall served as a hospital and as an occasional refuge for Confederate soldiers fleeing the enemy. Legend has it that Lizzie, who kept bees in the cupola, dressed the soldiers in bee suits and hid them there when she received word that the Yankees were coming. When the Union soldiers climbed the stairs to the cupola, she unleashed the bees, which drove the intruders back. Confederate soldiers were also secreted away in the hollow walls and the basement tunnel.

Not surprisingly, death is an important facet of the history of the Octagon Hall. Legend has it that two soldiers died at the house during the Civil War, one on the front steps and the other inside the house while being treated for his wounds. Both men were interred in the slave cemetery, which contains the graves of at least seventeen slaves. Several members of the Caldwell family are buried in the family cemetery on the property; some of them died in the house. Mary Elizabeth, Caldwell's daughter by his first wife, died when her dress caught fire in the kitchen. Caldwell himself succumbed to a bout of typhoid fever in the house in 1866.

The Octagon Hall remained in the Caldwell family until 1918, when the second wife sold it to Dr. Miles Williams. He occupied the Octagon Hall until he died in 1954. An assortment of renters lived in the house until 2010,

Visitors have seen ghostly soldiers sitting against a tree and standing in the driveway of the Octagon Hall. *Courtesy of Wikimedia Commons.*

when the Octagon Historical Society acquired the property and undertook an extensive restoration project. The house was listed in the National Register of Historic Places in 1980.

Owing to the abundance of reported paranormal events, the Octagon House is considered by members of the paranormal community to be one of the most haunted Civil War–era homes in the United States. Several years ago, a visitor saw the figure of a little girl in the yard from an upstairs window. The spirit of a little girl was also seen in the basement. The fragrant odor of flowers and the nauseating stench of rotting flesh have permeated the house on the anniversary of Andrew Jackson Caldwell's death. Local police have been summoned to the Octagon Hall late at night when the motion detectors are activated. When they arrived, officers found that the house was locked up and empty. A ghostly soldier was witnessed standing in the driveway. Another soldier was seen sitting on the ground, leaning against a tree. One can only surmise that he was either waiting for treatment or recovering in the fresh air of the outdoors.

Like many antebellum homes, the Octagon Hall has celebrated its haunted reputation by opening its doors to paranormal investigations. In fact, over 350 paranormal groups have conducted research inside the historic mansion. Video evidence collected by different paranormal groups includes a wheelchair moving by itself on the second floor and a glowing orb hovering over a candle for a brief time. A number of startling EVPs have been collected in the house as well, including the voice of a little girl saying, "Go to sleep" and "Mommy." A spectral knocking sound was recorded on the top floor. One of the most terrifying personal experiences occurred when a seven-foot-tall shadow figure attacked several investigators. Not everyone believes these stories, but enough do to make this historic home a favorite among ghost hunters.

Chapter 2

LEGENDARY BAD MEN

JESSE JAMES (BARDSTOWN)

Frank and Jesse James are usually associated with Missouri. However, they had some strong family connections with Kentucky. Their stepfather, Reuben Samuel, lived in Nelson County. Their cousin Mary Emma Graves lived in Chaplin with her husband, Thomas Sims Graves. Jesse was visiting his relatives in Chaplin when the Russellville bank was robbed in March 1868. Frank may have been in Chaplin at that time as well. Frank and a wartime friend, Alan Parmer, shot and killed two men near Chaplin who were accused of raping a woman in Nelson County. However, most of the legends dealing with Jesse James are based in Bardstown.

On October 18, 1881, Jesse was eating dinner in a roadhouse in Bardstown when a man marched in with a newspaper in hand, proclaiming that Jesse and his gang had just robbed a bank in Missouri. Jesse rose from the table and angrily declared that he was Jesse James, implying that he could not have robbed the bank in Missouri. He then walked over to a window and etched his name and the date—October 18, 1881—into the glass with his diamond ring to prove that he was not in Missouri when the robbery occurred. Fifty years later, when the roadhouse was demolished, the windowpane was taken to Florida and displayed in a case that was said to be earthquake-proof. The glass was eventually moved back to Bardstown and displayed in the Bardstown Historical Museum, but over time, it was misplaced, and a photograph of the pane of glass was displayed instead. The etching in the photograph is said to be more clearly visible than the one on the original windowpane, which is now on display in the Center for Kentucky History in Frankfort.

Jesse made his deepest impression in Kentucky on Bardstown's historic Old Talbott Tavern. Known as the oldest western stagecoach stop in America, the Old Talbott Tavern was built in 1779. With its Flemish bond stone walls and deep window casings, the building resembles the Warwickshire Inns in England. Until 1805, all of the male guests stayed in one of the rooms, and all of the female guests stayed in the other room. The tavern was ideally situated at the crossroads of western travel at that time. At the end of the eighteenth century, the Old Talbott Tavern served as a stop at the western end of the stagecoach road from Pennsylvania and Virginia. In the 1880s, the tavern expanded with the addition of a western wing of brick and a connecting wing with verandas. The most western part of the tavern, which originally housed a drugstore, was added in the 1960s. On March 7, 1998, the upstairs part of the building was damaged in an electrical fire, suffering mostly smoke and water damage. The restoration work was completed in November 1999.

Celebrities such as John James Audubon, William Henry Harrison and Abraham Lincoln have stayed at the Old Talbott Tavern, built in 1779.

After a hard night of drinking, Jesse James woke up and fired his pistol at the painted birds on the mural. The three bullet holes are still visible.

The legacies of old inns and hotels often include tales of visits by famous guests and surprise appearances by an intrusive specter or two. The Old Talbott Tavern is no exception. The guest list includes such notables as John James Audubon, Stephen Foster, William Henry Harrison and Abraham Lincoln. American presidents were not the only national leaders to spend time at the tavern. Louis Phillipe, the exiled king of France, left a lasting impression on Bardstown when he and his entourage booked a suite at the Old Talbott Tavern on October 17, 1797. Something more tangible than memories remained in the tavern after the king's departure. A series of stunning murals covered the walls of the upstairs room where the king and his party had spent the night. They were painted by a member of the king's entourage. The murals were uncovered in 1927.

A far less prestigious but equally famous visitor rented a room at the Old Talbott Tavern. Local legend has it that Jesse James took a break from robbing trains and banks to pay a call on his cousin Donnie Pence, who, ironically, was sheriff of Nelson County. The story goes that, one night, James returned to his room in the tavern to sleep off the whiskey he had imbibed that evening. Sometime during the night, he fired his pistol. Some say he was shooting at an intruder who may have been a ghost. Others say that he was shooting at some birds on the mural that appeared to be moving. The bullet holes in the wall bear mute witness to James's legendary stay at the Old Talbott Tavern.

The spirit of Jesse James is the historic inn's most famous ghost. A former bookkeeper at the inn had one of the most startling encounters with the

A server and a cook saw the ghost of a man in a long coat standing on the landing of the stairway in the Old Talbott Tavern.

outlaw's ghost. One night at closing time, she was taking the day's earnings to the safe upstairs when she was confronted by the figure of a man in a long coat walking across the top landing. A cook who had just emerged from the kitchen also saw the strangely dressed man. The women ran up the stairs to the second floor, where they saw the man walk through several rooms before leaving through the fire-escape door. Their curiosity overcame their sense of unease, and the women opened the door. Expecting him to have descended the stars, the women were surprised to find him standing on the landing, glaring them. Then, with a bloodcurdling laugh, he vanished. Three weeks later, the bookkeeper was watching a television special with her husband when a strangely familiar face appeared on the screen. Then it dawned on her that this was the face of the man she and the cook had seen on the landing: Jesse James. It turned out that two other employees have also seen the man with the long coat walking the hallways.

The ghost of Jesse James is not the only spirit haunting the Old Talbott Inn. Three years after George Talbott bought the inn in 1886, six of his children died there. Two of them died tragically, one by suicide and the other by falling. A lady who was staying in the General's Quarters Room reported to management that she had been awakened by a little girl kissing her. Mrs. Talbott's ghost is believed to be the "lady in white" who floats up the stairs and occasionally appears in the rooms. A couple who left in the middle of the night explained that they could not spend any more time at the inn, because they saw a lady in white standing over them. Suddenly, she floated out of the window.

Other types of ghostly activity have been reported at the Old Talbott Tavern. Televisions have been known to turn off. One guest saw multicolored orbs floating over his bed. Guests responding to a strange knocking at the door have been perplexed to find that no one is there. Disembodied footsteps and voices and ghostly piano playing have been reported as well. Jesse James may be gone, but in many ways, he has not really checked out.

Boone Helm: The Kentucky Cannibal (Lincoln)

Boone Helm was born in Lincoln, Kentucky, on January 28, 1827. His parents, Joseph and Eunice Helm, were regarded by their neighbors as good, hardworking people. Growing up, Boone exhibited a propensity for performing feats of strength and agility, such as sticking a bowie knife in the ground, then galloping toward it on horseback and grabbing it. His heavy drinking, which began when he was a teenager, may have been responsible for his angry outbursts. In 1848, when he was twenty years old, he married seventeen-year-old Lucinda Browning. She soon gave birth to a girl, Lucy. Helm's drinking led him to abuse his wife physically and to ride his horse into the house on occasion. Unable to tolerate her husband's alcohol-fueled rages, Lucinda filed for divorce. Helm's father covered the legal costs, but the bad publicity bankrupted him and ruined his reputation.

Like thousands of other Americans, Helm was drawn to the California Gold Rush in 1849. He invited his cousin Littlebury Shoot to join him. After a while, Shoot tired of the rigors of the journey and informed Helm that he was turning back. Helm responded to this bad news by stabbing his cousin in the chest and moving on to California. When Shoot's family members learned of his vicious murder, they tracked Helm down and turned him over to the authorities. Boone's erratic behavior convinced the judge that he should be committed to an asylum for the insane. Before long, though, Boone ran off while taking a walk in the woods with his guards. He then resumed his trek westward. Somewhere along the way, he grew into the habit of eating the bodies of the men he argued with and killed. To insulate himself from arrest, he joined up with six other men, all of whom soon learned of their new partner's cannibalism. The men were on the way to Fort Hall, Idaho, when they were attacked by a band of Indians. Forced to take refuge in the wilderness, the men were driven by hunger to eat their own horses. All of them died, with the exception of Helm and a man named Burton. Rather than face starvation, Burton shot himself. Helm staved off hunger by eating one of Burton's legs and packing the other one for the long trip to California.

After spending some time in an Indian camp, Helm made his way to Salt Lake City. Fearing arrest for his string of murders, Helm moved on to San Francisco. He murdered a rancher who had befriended him and hidden him from the law. Helm fled to Oregon, where he continued supporting himself by robbing and murdering those he met on the trail. Helm's shooting of an unarmed man, Dutch Fred, in a saloon in 1862 led to his arrest by the local sheriff. Helm's detention in the local lockup was short-lived, however. Before his trial, Helm's brother "Old Tex" bribed the witnesses, and the jury acquitted Helm of all charges. Helm went to Texas, then to Montana, robbing, killing and eating more victims on the way.

Helm's murderous career came to an abrupt end after he joined the Henry Plummer Gang. Shortly thereafter, he and four members of the gang were arrested by Montana vigilantes. In the trial that followed, Helm blamed all of his crimes on one of his cohorts, "Three Fingers" Jack Gallagher. All of the men were found guilty and hanged. Before Helm was hanged on January 14, 1864, he blessed Jefferson Davis, exclaimed "Let 'er rip!" and jumped off the hangman's box before the hangman could do his job.

ROD FERRELL: THE VAMPIRE CULT KILLER (MURRAY AND EUSTIS)

Born on March 28, 1980, Rod Ferrell was raised by his mother, Sondra Gibson, who supported herself and her son by working as a sex worker and an exotic dancer. Rod claimed that he was five years old when his maternal grandfather molested him, although no charges were ever filed in the case. For much of his childhood, Rod grew up in public housing in Murray and Eustis. As a teenager, he was infected with his mother's fascination with vampirism, especially role-playing games like Vampyre: The Masquerade and Dungeons and Dragons. An older boy named Stephen Murphy claimed to have initiated Rod into vampirism by involving him in blood-drinking rituals.

In 1994, Rod was expelled from Eustis High School as a ninth grader. His erratic behavior was aggravated by his increasing drug abuse. By the age of fifteen, he was using marijuana and lysergic acid diethylamide (LAD). Within a couple of years, Rod had moved on to heroin and cocaine. At this time, he frequently flew into drug-induced rages one minute and then plunged into deep depression the next. He blamed his lack of self-control on demonic possession.

Between the ages of fifteen and sixteen, Rod's life became a downward spiral. He claimed to be a five-hundred-year-old vampire named Vesago. He soon set about recruiting followers, such as Heather Wendorf, who claimed to have been abused by her parents. Ferrell's Vampire Coven, as it came to be known in the press, grew to twenty-five to thirty members. They conducted their satanic rituals and blood-drinking at an abandoned building they called the "Vampire Hotel."

Rod's antisocial antics first came to the attention of the authorities when he broke into the Murray-Calloway County Animal Shelter and tortured and killed two puppies. He was arrested and charged with trespassing, burglary and cruelty to animals. This incident proved to be just a precursor to worse things to come. On November 25, 1996, Ferrell and Scott Anderson entered Heather Wendorf's home in Florida to "save" her from her parents. Ferrell approached her father, Richard Wendorf, who was asleep on the couch, and bludgeoned him to death with a crowbar. Alerted by the noise coming from the living room, Heather's mother, Naoma Queen, confronted her husband's assailant, throwing scalding coffee in his face. He lunged at her and struck her on the head once with the crowbar, killing her instantly. Heather's seventeen-year-old sister, Jennifer, discovered the bodies. Heather did not find out about her parents' murder until several days later.

Ferrell and Anderson left the Wendorf house and joined up with Ferrell's sixteen-year-old girlfriend, Charity Keesee, and her nineteen-year-old friend Dana Cooper and headed to New Orleans, where there was an arcade that Ferrell liked. Four days later, Ferrell, Anderson and the two girls were apprehended by the police in Baton Rouge at a Howard Johnson's hotel. Following his arrest, Ferrell told reporters that he was being framed by a rival vampire coven and that he had multiple personalities. Following a sensational trial that was covered in the national media, Charity Keesee received a ten-year prison sentence; Dana Cooper was given a seventeen-year sentence.

Anderson's sentence was reduced to forty years. Ferrell was sentenced to death in the electric chair. However, in November 2000, his sentence was commuted to life in prison. Two grand juries found that Heather Wendorf was not complicit in the murder of her parents.

DONALD HARVEY: THE ANGEL OF DEATH (LONDON)

Donald Harvey was born on April 15, 1952, in Butler County, Ohio. He dropped out of school in the ninth grade, but he still managed to find a job as an orderly at the Marymount Hospital in London, Kentucky, in May 1970, when he was eighteen. During his ten-month stay at the hospital, he murdered at least twelve patients. He smothered two of them with pillows and hooked up ten others to oxygen tanks that were nearly empty. Although he insisted that he killed them to relieve them of their suffering, Harvey admitted that he murdered some of them out of anger. The death count was so high that Harvey's coworkers called him the "Angel of Death."

Harvey's career as a hospital orderly was briefly interrupted when he was arrested for burglary on March 31, 1971. He pled guilty and was urged by the judge to undergo psychiatric treatment, but Harvey enlisted in the U.S. Air Force instead. He was discharged in March 1972 and returned to Kentucky for unknown reasons. His mental instability led to his being committed to the Veterans Administration Medical Center from July 16 to August 25 and from September 17 to October 17, 1972. The multiple electroshock treatments he received resulted in little improvement in his behavior. In Lexington, Harvey worked part-time as a nurse's aide at Cardinal Hill Hospital from February to August 1973. He then moved on to Lexington's Good Samaritan Hospital, where he worked through January 1974. While working as a telephone operator in Lexington and as a clerk at St. Luke's Hospital in Fort Thomas between August 1974 and September 1975, he found it more difficult to suppress his desire to commit "mercy killings."

In January 1975, Harvey moved from Kentucky and found work at the Cincinnati VA Medical Center, where he held a variety of different positions. While working as an autopsy assistant, Harvey occasionally took home body parts "for study." During the next ten years, he "euthanized" at least fifteen patients he perceived to be in great pain, occasionally poisoning them. His patients were not his only victims, however. An admitted homosexual, he poisoned his lover and roommate, Carl, because he believed him to be unfaithful. He also poisoned two of his neighbors, Diane Alexander and

Helen Metzger. In July 1985, Harvey was fired from the VA Medical Center when security guards examined a satchel he was carrying and discovered hypodermic needles, surgical scissors, gloves, a cocaine spoon, a .38-caliber pistol and two books of occult lore. He was unemployed for only seven months when he was hired as a part-time nurse's aide at Cincinnati's Drake Memorial Hospital. Over the next thirteen months, he poisoned twenty-three additional patients. Harvey's crimes finally came to light on March 7, 1987, when the death of one of his patients, John Powell, was ruled murder by cyanide. Following his arrest in April, Harvey pled not guilty to the charge of murder. He went on to confess to thirty-three additional murders, and new charges were filed on August 11, 1987. Seven days later, he confessed to twenty-four murders and received four consecutive twenty-years-to-life sentences. On September 7, 1987, Harvey confessed to taking the lives of twelve patients at Marymount Hospital. After pleading guilty to three more murders in Cincinnati, Harvey was given three life sentences. In 1991, Harvey told an interviewer that he "played God" by appointing himself judge, prosecutor and jury. The Associated Press named him the worst serial killer in the United States on July 23, 2001. Harvey was attacked and beaten to death in his prison cell in 2017.

The Harp Brothers: Hell Comes to Kentucky (Webster County)

The annals of Kentucky history are filled with the exploits of bloodthirsty scoundrels who rode wild and free in the early years of the state. Two of the worst of these bad men were the Harp brothers, Micajah (Big Harp) and Wiley (Little Harp). Following the Revolutionary War, the Harps were forced to flee to East Tennessee, because their father was a Tory who fought for the British. After taking up with two sisters, Susan and Betsy Roberts, the brothers moved to Knox County, not far from Knoxville, in 1795.

For two years, the Harps ranged through Tennessee in the company of Indians, leaving a bloody trail behind them as they robbed travelers and stole cattle. One of their victims, a man named Johnson, was found in the Holston River. His chest was cut open and filled with large rocks. This became the brothers' modus operandi for many years to come.

As the outlaws made their way through the Cumberland Gap, they were joined by another woman, Sally Rice. Not long after their arrival in

Kentucky in December 1798, the Harps murdered a peddler and stole his horse and wares. They then went to Lincoln County, where they befriended a couple of travelers named Pacca and Bates. After a while, the Harps shot their traveling companions. Pacca tried to get up, but Big Harp finished him off with a tomahawk. Later, they made the acquaintance of a man named Langford in a tavern in Rockcastle County. When Langford's body was discovered a few days later, the Harps were captured near Crab Orchard. While waiting for trial in Danville, the brothers broke out of jail on March 16, 1799. Their women had been jailed along with their babies. After the women were tried and acquitted, the citizens of Danville gave them money and clothing for their journey. They met up with the Harps one hundred miles away near Diamond Island in Henderson County. A group of regulators under the command of Josh Ballinger tracked the Harps to Rolling Fort, but the brothers managed to escape.

Not long after Governor James Garrard offered a $300 reward for the capture of either of the brothers on April 22, 1799, the Harps killed a man named Dooley in Metcalf County and another named Stump below Bowling Green. A regulator named Captain Young set about to rid Kentucky of the Harps and all of the other land pirates in the area, including a man named Samuel Mason, who led the brothers across the Ohio River to his hideout in Cave-in Rock. The Harps used Cave-in Rock as their base of operations until being expelled for forcing a captive and his blindfolded horse to ride off a cliff.

The Harps had no choice but to pass through Kentucky on their way back to the Knoxville area. In July 1799, they killed two men near Knoxville: a farmer named Bradbury and another man named Harding. They also murdered a boy from Coffee for the sole purpose of taking his gun. After killing William Ballard, the Harps encountered two brothers, James and Robert Brasel. They wounded James severely and cut his throat, but Robert ran off. As the Harps neared the Tennessee-Kentucky border, they killed John Tully. When they came upon Tully's son a little later, they murdered him, too. In August 1799, the brothers murdered a young Black boy and a girl who were out picking berries. The Harps' bloodlust reached such a fever pitch that Big Harp even killed his own baby, smashing it against a tree. The child's only crime was crying incessantly. Later on, Big Harp confessed that this was the only murder he ever regretted.

The Harps assumed new identities when they returned to Kentucky. Ironically, they disguised themselves as Methodist ministers. One night, the brothers stopped over at the home of an acquaintance of theirs, Moses

Stegall. He was out of town, so his wife, Mary, fed them and allowed them to stay at their home. Big Harp was sleeping in the same room with another guest, Major William Love. In the middle of the night, Big Harp's roommate started snoring, so Harp bashed him in the head with a tomahawk. The next night, Mrs. Stegall's baby kept Big Harp up with her crying, so he cut her throat. The ruckus woke Mrs. Stegall, and she rushed into Big Harp's room. As she stood there, screaming, Big Harp killed her as well. Fearing the wrath of Moses Stegall, the Harps fled. The next morning, they approached the campsite of two men, Gilmore and Hudgens. The Harps shot and killed Gilmore immediately. Hudgens took off, but the Harps caught him and murdered him as well.

Meanwhile, Moses Stegall had returned home, expecting to be warmly greeted by his wife and baby. The sight of the bodies of his wife and child lying on the floor in a pool of blood turned his stomach and brought tears to his eyes. When he regained composure, Stegall organized a posse to bring the murderers to justice. The vigilantes caught up with the Harps, just as they were about to murder and rob a man named George Smith. As the

Big Harp and Little Harp joined the Mason Gang at their hideout in Cave-In Rock. *Courtesy of Wikimedia Commons.*

brothers were trying to ride off, one of the men shot Big Harp in the leg and the back and dragged him off of his horse. Paralyzed, Big Harp confessed to twenty murders. At the end of his confession, Moses Stegall slowly cut off his head with a butcher knife. Legend has it that Harp was still alive as Stegall decapitated him. His head was stuck on a pole that was placed at a crossroads near Henderson, Kentucky, as a warning to other outlaws. Big Harp is rumored to have buried $300,000 in gold somewhere near the road that bears his name, Harp's Head Road, near Dixon.

Instead of trying to defend his brother when the shooting began, Little Harp rode off and sought refuge with the Mason Gang at Cave-in Rock. Using the alias John Sutton, Little Harp fit in with the other outlaws, robbing and killing anyone they encountered for four years. One day, Little Harp found out that a hefty reward was being offered for Samuel Mason's head. Lured by the prospect of a big payday, Little Harp and another river pirate, James May, murdered the leader of their gang and delivered his head to the authorities. However, their notoriety preceded them; one of the officers recognized them and arrested them. Little Harp and May escaped but were recaptured shortly thereafter. They were hanged in January 1804, and their heads were stuck on high stakes along the Natchez Road. Travelers and settlers in Kentucky, Mississippi and Tennessee breathed a lot easier after the horrible Harp brothers took their last breaths. Their murders of over forty men, women and children earned them the title "America's First Serial Killers."

Chapter 3

LEGENDARY CEMETERIES

CAVE HILL CEMETERY (LOUISVILLE)

Cave Hill Cemetery is located on a section of the William Johnston family farm that was known as Cave Hill, although the farm's most valuable geographical features were its quarries. Over time, the family's old brick house was converted into the City Pest House, where people suffering from a variety of contagious diseases were treated. The cemetery itself was not established on the property until 1846. The mayor and the city council hired a civil engineer named Edmund Francis Lee (1811–1857) to design a garden cemetery that made use of the land's natural features. Graves were dug on the tops of hills. Trees were planted in some of the basins. Other basins were filled with water to create ponds. Lee's vision of transforming a burial ground into a park where citizens could relax was finally realized on July 25, 1848, when Cave Hill Cemetery was dedicated by Reverend Doctor Edward Porter Humphrey. During the Civil War, burial plots were sold for both Union and Confederate soldiers. In 1888, the size of the cemetery was expanded to three hundred acres. Today, the stream flowing out of Cave Hill divides the cemetery into eastern and western sections. A number of celebrities are buried at Cave Hill Cemetery, including George Rogers Clark, Muhammad Ali, Colonel Harland Sanders and Patty and Mildred J. Hill, who composed "Happy Birthday."

This is the entrance to Cave Hill Cemetery, which was founded on a section of the William Johnston family farm.

Civil engineer Edmund Francis Lee used the natural features of the landscape when he designed Cave Hill Cemetery.

The ghost of Colonel Harland Sanders has been seen wandering around his grave.

Cave Hill Cemetery is believed to be one of the most haunted cemeteries in Kentucky. Not surprisingly, most of the paranormal activity seems to take place at night. When a full moon hangs in the sky, people have reported hearing chanting and disembodied footsteps inside the cemetery. Green orbs have been sighted floating around the graves. These glowing balls of light have been captured in photographs as well. Flickering objects appear and disappear on occasion. Apparitions, such as the ghost of Colonel Harland Sanders, have been known to walk around the cemetery. A few visitors claim to have been watched by a pair of glowing eyes. The claim can clearly be made that not all of the spirits in Cave Hill Cemetery are "resting in peace."

ROWAN FAMILY CEMETERY, FEDERAL HILL: MY OLD KENTUCKY HOME STATE PARK (BARDSTOWN)

The mansion known as Federal Hill was designed by Judge John Rowan and his wife, Ann Lytle. The ell portion was constructed in 1795; the main block was finished in 1818 with slave labor. It was constructed on a native limestone foundation and with a brick exterior. The main rooms are on the first floor. The kitchen and the smokehouse can be found in the ell section. In 1839, a fire did considerable damage to the third story and the roof. A number of celebrities visited the Federal-style mansion, including Andrew Jackson, Henry Clay and the Marquis de Lafayette. According to Stephen Foster's biographers, the story that Foster visited the mansion and based his song "My Old Kentucky Home" on Federal Hill has been heavily disputed. Federal Hill was designated a State Historic Site in 1936. It was renovated in 1977 and 2006. Today, the state park's main attractions are the mansion itself and John Rowan's tombstone in the family cemetery.

John Rowan was born on July 12, 1773. When he was a child, he and his family moved to Kentucky from Pennsylvania. They settled in Bardstown, where Rowan read law under George Nicholas. Rowan married Anne Lyttle in October 1973 after completing his legal training. He and Anne purchased the land that was to become Federal Hill farm with money he received from Anne's father. The couple had a total of nine children. As

Judge John Rowan built Federal Hill between 1795 and 1818.

The ghost of John Rowan expresses his disapproval of his grave marker by pushing it down.

his family grew, Rowan became increasingly aware of the need to build a bigger house. After it was completed, John and Anne named it Federal Hill, after the Federal political party.

Rowan's career was sidetracked by an argument that ensued during a card game. Rowan and Dr. James Chambers became involved in a physical brawl and agreed to duel it out two days later. On February 3, Rowan shot Chambers in the chest. Rowan apologized and tried to get Chambers medical assistance. Before he died the next day, Chambers implored his friends not to prosecute John Rowan.

Rowan's political career blossomed in the first half of the nineteenth century, despite his shooting Chambers. He was appointed Kentucky's secretary of state in 1823 and was elected to the U.S. Senate a year later. He held that position until 1830, when he returned to Kentucky, where he was chosen as the first president of the Louisville Medical Institute. Until his death on July 12, 1843, Rowan and his family lived part of the time at Federal Hill and the rest of the time at their townhouse in Louisville.

Before his death, Rowan had requested that no stone marker or monument be placed on his grave, because his parents' graves had no such markers. He wanted Federal Hill to serve as his monument. However, his family disregarded his last wishes, insisting that a man of his prominence deserved a fitting memorial. A tall obelisk was mounted on his grave. He was buried in the Rowan family cemetery, which is also known as Federal Hill Cemetery, not far from his home. Just a few days later, his tombstone toppled over. The stonemasons who were summoned to reset the marker said that tree roots must have caused it to tip over. Almost two months later, the obelisk fell again. Several of the stonemasons refused to come to the cemetery because of rumors that were spreading about John Rowan's restless spirit. Over time, no stonemasons would reset the tombstone, so caretakers assumed the task of resetting it every time it fell over. Locals say that Rowan's ghost is still expressing its displeasure by knocking over his tombstone.

The facts behind the legend of John Rowan's obelisk may have come to light in 2021. During the first week of June, the staff at Federal Hill received a scrapbook from descendants of the Rowan family. Inside the scrapbook was evidence that a stone urn placed on top of the obelisk, not the obelisk itself, had a tendency to fall over.

THE GRAVE IN HARRODSBURG SPRINGS PARK (HARRODSBURG)

In the 1840s, Harrodsburg gained fame as a resort town. People traveled from hundreds of miles away to drink the water from its mineral springs. Many of them stayed at the Harrodsburg Springs Hotel on the edge of town. The owners, Dr. and Mrs. C.C. Graham, went to great expense to ensure that their hotel catered to all of their guests' needs. Its most prominent feature was the ballroom, whose mirrored walls reflected the light from over one hundred chandeliers. Dr. Graham trained the servants who made up the band that accompanied the dances. One of the young ladies who participated in the dances arrived by carriage late one summer afternoon with only one piece of luggage. Other guests at the hotel recalled that her long hair was piled up on her head and hung down the sides of her face in ringlets. She registered as Virginia Stafford and told the desk clerk that her parents would arrive later in the evening with the rest of her luggage. She then went to her room and got dressed for the ball. When she entered the ballroom an hour later, she was surrounded by more than a dozen young men who begged her for the privilege of dancing with her. After dancing for almost an hour, she walked outside during intermission with several of her admirers. While a mockingbird sang, the girl stared at the moon and exclaimed, "Oh, I am so happy! I wish I could stay here forever and ever." When the last dance was called, she glided around the floor with her last partner. When the music ended, she fell into his arms. She was dead.

It turned out that all of the personal information she had given at the desk was false. An examination of her personal belongings produced no clue as to her death. Newspapers ran a story about "the Girl who danced herself to death." Her dancing partners served as her pallbearers. She was buried at the spot where she listened to the mockingbird's song in the hotel's backyard. Her grave was marked "Unknown." When the hotel burned to the ground in the 1920s, blame was placed on the ghost of the dead girl. Not long after the fire, reports began to surface of the ghost of a young girl dancing by her grave and the springhouse. Once the area became Harrodsburg Springs Park, the number of sightings increased. One eyewitness was a nurse who was walking through the park at midnight in the 1960s when she saw a young woman in an old-fashioned white gown walking toward her from the springhouse. As the girl came closer, she said, "I'm lost. I can't find the hotel. Can you please help me?" When the nurse replied that the hotel burned down years before, the girl ran back to the springhouse, crying, and disappeared.

GRANDVIEW CEMETERY/KASEY CEMETERY (ELIZABETHTOWN)

Grandview Cemetery is located west of Elizabethtown on a remote country road. The origin of the cemetery is a mystery. Several of the tombstones date prior to the founding of Elizabethtown in 1795. The cemetery may have been founded by the Kasey family, whose graves are among the oldest in the cemetery. Some locals have speculated that the cemetery may have been a family homestead at some point in its history. The mystery is amplified by the stories told about strange things that have occurred there, such as a large green orb that hovered over the ground before flying into the air. Shadow figures have been seen here as well. Visitors to the cemetery have reported bleeding from their nose and mouth and hearing bloodcurdling screams from the middle of the cemetery. Some people have had trouble starting

Grandview Cemetery was founded by the Kasey family, whose graves are some of the oldest in the burial ground.

Visitors to the cemetery have had nosebleeds, heard bloodcurdling screams and seen orbs flitting around the tombstones.

The graveyard is known as the "Gates of Hell Cemetery" because of the satanic rites that some say have been performed here.

their cars after walking through the cemetery. A few people claim to have begun speaking in strange languages as they walk through the graves. Some people have been overcome by feelings of sadness. Orbs and black patches of grass appear at random times in the cemetery as well.

Grandview Cemetery is also known as the "Gates of Hell Cemetery." This unfortunate nickname stems from the rumors of satanic rituals that are said to have been performed here. In 2003, Kentucky State Police discovered the mutilated remains of cats, dogs, deer and a calf inside the cemetery. No charges of animal cruelty were filed in this particular case, but many other cases of animal sacrifice have been reported here over the years. In fact, so many animals have been killed here that some locals call it "the killing field." According to one local legend, the sacrifices are made to appease a witch who lurks around the woods. One can expect one of the oldest cemeteries in Kentucky to have spawned rumors, but the legends people tell about Grandview Cemetery are particularly sinister.

BAKER'S HOLLOW ROAD CEMETERY (MARION)

Hellhounds are legendary beasts that probably had their origins with Cerberus, the three-headed dog that guards the gates of Hades in Greek mythology. In 1577, a monstrous black canine known as "Black Shuck" attacked the members of Bungay Church in Suffolk, England. He then moved on to Holy Trinity Church, where he not only murdered a man and his son but even caused the steeple to topple off the roof. The appearance in England of a headless hellhound called the "Yeth Hound," which usually travels only at night, is considered by many to be an omen of death. Kentucky's version of the hellhound is said to be found at Baker's Hollow Road Cemetery in Marion.

Baker's Hollow Road Cemetery is one of two cemeteries that make up the Baker-Phillips Cemetery. Located to the side of Baker Church, Baker Cemetery is the church's official burial ground; Phillips Cemetery, located in front of the church, is the burial ground for members of the Phillips family. The Baker-Phillips Cemetery can be found on Baker Church Road. For years, locals have been lured to Baker's Hollow Road Cemetery by the legend of the hellhound, a large black dog with glowing yellow eyes. According to the blog *Theresa's Haunted History of the Tri-State*, the dog is able to keep up with cars that drive away from the cemetery, even though it appears to be limping. When the dog reaches the *Y* in the road, it transforms into a demonic beast and vanishes. Theresa says that the story of the cemetery's black dog may be a product of the folk belief, prevalent in the southern United States, that the first person to be buried in a new cemetery may return in the form of a creature to serve as its guardian.

THE WITCH GIRL OF PILOT KNOB CEMETERY (MARION)

Pilot Knob Cemetery has acquired a mysterious, if not sinister, reputation over the years. Located in Marion, Kentucky, on Pilot Knob Cemetery Road, the little burial ground is said to be shunned by locals, who are keeping the legend of the Witch Girl alive. They say that outsiders often ask directions to the cemetery because "there is a lot of stuff that goes on up there." This is definitely one of those tales that does not hold up to close scrutiny.

According to the standard version of the tale, a six-year-old-girl named Mary Evelyn Ford was living with her mother in Marion in the early 1900s.

The rumors that the mother and daughter were witches fueled the fears of some of the townsfolk. One night, an angry mob murdered them using the traditional method of disposing of witches—they burned them to death. Mrs. Ford was buried miles from Marion; Mary's charred remains were buried in a steel-lined grave covered with concrete. A layer of gravel was spread on top of her grave, which was enclosed in a white fence made of interconnecting crosses. These precautions were taken to prevent her unquiet spirit from taking revenge on the town.

For years, the citizens of Marion stayed clear of her grave out of fear that she would grab anyone who ventured too close. Some say that her ghost makes faces at onlookers in an attempt to make them so angry that they will walk close enough for her to reach up and pull them into the grave with her. Some visitors claim to have seen the ghost of a little blond girl in a white nightgown walking around the inside perimeter of the fence.

According to *Theresa's Haunted History of the Tri-State*, Mary Evelyn Ford was the daughter of Mary Rebecca Davis Ford and James Andy Ford. Mary contracted peritonitis and died just before her fifth birthday on May 31, 1975. Mrs. Ford died in 1955 and was interred in the same cemetery. The witch story seems to have been created to keep trespassers out of the cemetery. However, like many cautionary tales, this one seems to have had the opposite effect, especially for young people eager to test their courage by visiting her grave at night.

Chapter 4

LEGENDARY CHARACTERS

DANIEL BOONE (BOONESBOROUGH)

With the possible exception of Davy Crockett, Daniel Boone was the most iconic frontiersman in American history. Like Crockett, Boone was truly a legend in his own time; in fact, many tall tales were being told about him when he was still alive. Although Boone will always be associated primarily with Kentucky, several other states have claimed him as well. He was born on November 2, 1734, in Oley Valley, Berks County, Pennsylvania. His father, Squire Boone, had immigrated to colonial Pennsylvania from Bradninch, England, in 1713. At the time of Boone's birth, this part of Pennsylvania was untamed frontier, populated mostly by Indians and wild animals. Boone received little formal education. He was much more interested in learning how to track, hunt and survive in the wilderness. He learned even more about the Appalachian Mountains during the two years he served in the British army fighting against the French in the French and Indian War (1754–63). He began driving a wagon for General Edward Braddock in his effort to drive the French out of Ohio.

On August 14, 1756, Boone married Rebecca Bryan. They moved into a cabin on his father's farm in the Yadkin Valley. By this time, Boone had acquired the hunting skills to provide for his family. Over the span of their marriage, Rachel gave birth to ten children. Boone and his wife also took care of eight children belonging to family members who had died. When the Cherokee Indians began attacking the cabins of British colonists in the Yadkin Valley, Boone relocated his family to Culpepper County, Virginia.

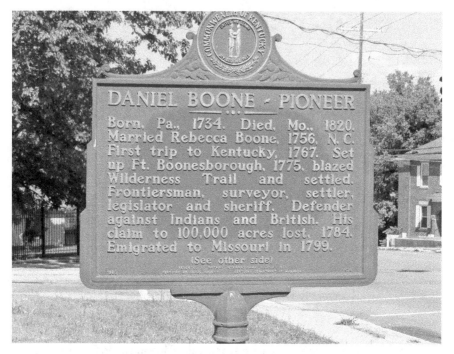

The Daniel Boone Pioneer Marker, erected in Frankfort in 1963, commemorates the exploits of Kentucky's most famous trailblazer. *Courtesy of Wikimedia Commons.*

Boone was already thinking of moving again after his father died in 1765 because the increasing number of settlers was driving the game out of the county. He considered moving to Florida and even traveled there to look for a suitable place to live. But in 1767, he decided to explore the possibility of living in Kentucky instead. He and his brother Squire went there but were unable to find the rich hunting grounds he had heard about. He made another trip to Kentucky two years later with a friend of his, but they were captured by Shawnee Indians, who drove them out after stealing their skins. On September 25, 1773, Boone sold his farm and led his family and five other families to Kentucky for the purpose of putting down roots there, but they turned back after his eldest son, James, was captured and tortured by the Shoshone Indians in Dunmore's War. Kentucky was opened to colonization in 1775, after a friend of Boone's, Richard Henderson, made treaties with the Indians. He hired Boone to blaze a trail with a group of thirty men through the Cumberland Gap to the Kentucky River on the Wilderness Road. They brought along a number of slaves as well.

When the men reached the fertile grounds of Kentucky, they set about constructing a twelve-foot-high stockade they called Boonesborough. Boone was unknown before making the trek to Kentucky, but he became famous after rescuing his daughter Jemima and two other girls from a party of Shawnee. During the Siege of Boonesborough in 1778, Boone was shot in the ankle outside of the fort. A close friend of his, Simon Kenton, dragged the frontiersman inside. Afterward, Boone promised the Shawnee chief Blackfish that Boonesborough would surrender within a year. He was then adopted into the tribe but was able to escape several months later and return to the fort and warn the inhabitants of an impending attack by Blackfish.

After bringing his family back to Kentucky from North Carolina in 1779, Boone settled in Boone's Station, not far from Boonesborough. At this time, he became involved in the Revolutionary War when he joined George Rogers Clark's march into the Ohio country in 1780. During this campaign, his brother Ned was captured and beheaded by the Shawnees, probably because they mistook him for Daniel Boone.

After the Revolutionary War, he moved his family to Limestone, Kentucky, with the intention of settling down to the life of a businessman. At first, Daniel enjoyed success as a horse trader and land speculator. However, he lost most of the 100,000 acres he owned to swindlers. He moved once again, this time to Missouri in 1799, to start all over again. With the exception of a six-month trapping expedition up the Missouri River, he spent most of his doing a little hunting and spending time with his children and grandchildren. Daniel Boone died on September 26, 1820.

Because of Daniel Boone's status as a folk hero during his lifetime, it is somewhat difficult to separate truth from legend. One of the earliest stories told about him was set in his boyhood, when he is said to have built himself a rude hut out of logs a short distance from his home. People said he lived there for days at a time with his rifle, roaming the woods and hunting game. One probably apocryphal tale that was generated by Boone's lack of formal education is a statement his father made to his schoolteacher: "Let the girls do the spelling, and Dan will do the shooting." The truth is that Boone may have been a hunter and explorer, but he was not a dim-witted primitive. He enjoyed reading so much that he often read books like *Gulliver's Travels* aloud to his hunting companions around the campfire. He may have dressed like an Indian much of the time, but people who know him said that he was always "well-groomed." Also, Boone was not really a rough backwoodsman who turned his back on society. His biographers played up the popular notion that he moved over the mountains when he was able to see the smoke of a neighbor's chimney. Actually, Boone was very much a part of "civilized society" in Kentucky. Not only was he a lieutenant colonel in the Kentucky Militia, but he was also a representative in the Virginia General Assembly.

His early forays into the wilderness are believed to have prepared him for the life of a frontiersman who preferred the woods over the city. The image of Daniel Boone as a simple frontier rustic was popularized by a number of writers. In 1813, his nephew Daniel Bryan wrote a book-length poem about his uncle, *The Mountain Muse*. Boone himself branded it a "disaster of inaccuracy." Another idealized portrait of Boone as simple and authentic can be found in Lord Byron's 1823 poem *Don Juan*, in which he depicts Boone as a natural man who "shrank from men, even of his nation / When they built up unto his darling trees." However, the primary source of the romanticized depiction of Daniel Boone is *The Discovery, Settlement, and Present State of Kentucke* (1783) by a Pennsylvania schoolteacher named John Filson, who portrayed him as the embodiment of the "Noble Savage," a man who was honest and pure of society because he grew up close to nature.

The historical record also refutes the image of Boone as an iron-willed hero who thrust himself into the fray. Just before his marriage to Rebecca Bryan on August 7, 1756, he fled with other retreating soldiers following General Edward Braddock's defeat at the Battle of the Monongahela in the French and Indian War. This incident suggests that he did not conform to the traditional image of the heroic warrior. Indeed, he seems to have subscribed to the belief that, sometimes, withdrawing from a battle is the most prudent thing to do, living to fight another day. People who knew Boone swore that he hated bloodshed. Contrary to his reputation as an Indian-hating backwoodsman, he probably killed no more than three Indians, even going so far as saying that they were kinder to him than Whites were.

An aura of mystery surrounds his Rebecca Bryan as well. The story goes that Boone first met her one night while he was hunting. People say that she was briefly hypnotized by the glow of his firebrand and stood fixed to the spot. He did not realize that she was a girl until she awoke and ran off. Boone chased her down and instantly fell in love with her. Because he almost shot the girl of his dreams, Boone stopped hunting by the light of a torch. In a variant of the tale, she was a shape-shifter who took the form of a deer the night Boone went hunting. During their courtship, Boone and Rebecca were sitting next to each other after picking cherries. To mask his nervousness, Boone began playing mumblety-peg and accidentally made several cuts in her apron. Boone's children said that he cut her apron on purpose to see what kind of temper she had. After Boone and Rebecca were married, she often had to go hunting, because her husband was gone for months at a time. As a result, she had to become an expert shot. One day, she climbed a tree on Deep Creek and shot seven deer and Rebecca's mare. Some say she was almost as good with a rifle as her husband was. She became the epitome of the frontier woman who found the strength to take over the farm while her man was gone. A tale that Boone's early biographers chose not to publish concerns one of her pregnancies. Supposedly, Boone returned home one day after an absence of several months to find that his wife was pregnant. She explained that she took up with his brother because she feared that Boone was dead. Instead of flying into a rage, Boone not only forgave Rebecca, but he also loved the child as if she were his own daughter. Present-day biographers have dismissed this story as nothing more than legend.

Of course, many of the Daniel Boone legends focus on his prowess as a hunter. One of the best-known spots in the Yadkin Valley is Bear Creek, which is said to have gotten its name from the ninety-one bears that he shot there. Because bears were hunted primarily for food at that time, this tale might be true. The story that Boone carved his name into a tree after a hunt would not have been unusual. Many hunters in the frontier celebrated a successful hunt this way. One tree that he carved his name on died and fell down near Jonesboro, Tennessee, in 1920. Another "Boone" tree was discovered near Johnson City, Tennessee. A beech tree bearing the carved inscription "D. Boon cilled a Bar in the year 1760" once stood on the Watauga River in Tennessee. The Filson Historical Society in Louisville, Kentucky, displays a carving that reads, "D. Boon Kilt a Bar, 1803." Because Boone often left the final "e" off of his name, carvings like this one are probably not fakes.

One of the most famous folktales about Daniel Boone is a hunting story recounted by Mary Hamilton in her book *Kentucky Folktales: Revealing Stories, Truths, and Outright Lies* (2012). Daniel Boone was out hunting one day when he was charged by a bear that was about fifty yards away. He was not hunting bear that particular day, so he climbed a nearby tree. He then sat on a limb with his back to the tree. He wrapped his legs around the tree trunk and hung down with his arms dangling. As soon as the bear began climbing up the tree after him, Boone stretched out his arm and stuck it inside the bear's mouth, all the way to the end of the bear. He then grabbed the tail and gradually pulled the bear inside out. Terrified by what had happened to him, the inside-out bear backed down the tree and vanished into the woods.

The term *legendary* is sometimes applied to achievements of his that are unbelievable because of their difficulty. The 200-mile trail that he and thirty companions cut through the Cumberland Gap is one of these amazing feats.

Equally impressive is his escape from Blackfish when he found out that the Shawnee were preparing an attack on Boonesborough. After eluding his captors, he managed to make the 160-mile trek back to Boonesborough in five days. Instead of giving up after his horse dropped dead from exhaustion, he completed the journey on foot. The historical record bears out the fact that he was an extraordinary man.

Not surprisingly, his death is shrouded in an aura of mystery. On September 26, 1820, his son Nathan buried him in an unmarked grave next to Rebecca's unmarked grave on Femme Osage Creek, Missouri. Markers were placed on the graves in the 1830s. Daniel and Rebecca were exhumed in 1845 and moved to a new cemetery in Frankfort, Kentucky. Not long thereafter, rumors circulated that Boone's grave marker in Missouri was placed on the wrong grave; therefore, his remains never left Missouri. According to legend, Boone's relatives knew that a mistake had been made, but they kept quiet because they did not want Boone's remains to be moved to Kentucky. Possible substantiation for this story emerged in 1983, when a forensic anthropologist examined a plaster cast made of Boone's skull. He concluded that the skull could have been that of an African American, probably a slave. Despite this evidence, both cemeteries claim to be the final resting place of Daniel Boone.

Not only has Daniel Boone's fame endured long after his death, but so has his ghost, at least, according to folklore. According to an article published in the *Louisville Courier-Journal* on August 31, 1984, Henry Clay's family was inside the conservatory of their home one night during a thunderstorm when a tall, lanky figure suddenly appeared: "The unbidden guest was grizzled and weather-beaten and with a grim visage. On his head he wore the historic coonskin, and his raiment was of buckskin from neck to moccasin. He carried one of the six-foot rifles used a hundred years ago and a powder-horn of huge size and antique appearance hung at his side. The family assumed that he was a wanderer from the mountains who was seeking shelter from the storm. They were puzzled, however, by his clothing, which was clearly from the previous century. He walked across the room and set his rifle in a corner. The night visitor then sat down in a chair across from Henry Clay's writing desk. Eager to dispel the unease that had swept across the room, Clay faced to the man and said, 'Friend, it's a wet night to be out,' but the strange man stared Clay in the face and gave no reply. After a few moments, the man picked up his rifle and vanished. Two male members of the Clay family immediately began searching for the weird man. They soon determined that no one could have simply walked into

The bodies of David and Rebecca Boone are believed to have been moved from their grave at Femme Osage Creek in Missouri to another grave in Frankfort, Kentucky. *Courtesy of Wikimedia Commons.*

the home because all of the doors and windows were securely locked. They were equally bewildered by the absence of water in the corner where the man had set his wet rifle." Henry Clay refused to discuss the strange incident afterwards, preferring to pretend that it had not happened. Clay's family, on the other hand, viewed the appearance of the apparition as an omen that someone in the Clay family was about to die. No one in the Clay family was very surprised when Henry Clay died shortly thereafter. They believed that the old man had been visited by the ghost of his old friend, Daniel Boone, and had followed him into the afterlife.

Daniel Boone's legacy extends far beyond the opening of the mountainous region beyond the Cumberland Gap to thousands of settlers. He also established Boonesborough as a bastion of Anglo civilization. Over the years, however, he has become an integral part of American culture. Many literary scholars believe that James Fenimore Cooper's iconic frontier character Hawkeye was modeled after Daniel Boone. A boys' organization called the Sons of Daniel Boone was the forerunner of the Boy Scouts of America.

The bicentennial of his birth was memorialized with the issuing of a half-dollar coin in 1934. He was portrayed in the 1936 film *Daniel Boone* and in the NBC television series *Daniel Boone* (1964–70). As the very embodiment of the frontier spirit, Daniel Boone's influence is likely to continue for many years to come.

THE BLUE FUGATES OF KENTUCKY (HAZARD)

In the early 1820s, a French orphan named Martin Fugate married a woman named Elizabeth. They built a home at Troublesome Creek. Like most couples at this time, they had a large family. Unlike most couples, however, four of their children were blue. Martin and Elizabeth Fugate did not realize that both of them were carriers of a recessive gene (met-H) that causes methemoglobinemia. Many people possessing this genetic trait are born with blue skin. For 150 years, generations of Fugates were born with a blue tint to their skin, not just because of their genetic makeup, but also because they lived in a very isolated, rural area, increasing the possibility that they would intermarry. Martin and Elizabeth's son Zachariah married his mother's sister. Their children married other Fugate cousins with names like Combs, Ritchie and Smith. Even though Zachariah and his wife were not blue, many of their descendants were.

The complexion of the Fugate family began to change after the railroad came to the region in 1910. Over time, more and more members of the family began leaving the area, giving them more opportunities to marry outside of their family. As a result, fewer and fewer descendants of Martin Fugate were born with a blue tinge to their skin. In the early 1960s, a hematologist at the University of Kentucky's Lexington Medical Clinic, Dr. Madison Cawein III, injected two of Martin Fugate's blue descendants with methylene. Before long, their blue skin color began to fade away. The couple kept their disorder in check by taking methylene. Dr. Cawein published the results of his study in the *Archives of Internal Medicine* in 1964.

The last known descendant of the Fugates to have blue skin was Benjamin Stacy, born in 1975. However, his blue skin tone quickly faded as he aged. Eventually, only his lips and fingertips displayed a blue tinge, usually when he was agitated or cold. After six generations, the blue legacy of Martin Fugate seemed to have come to an end.

EDGAR CAYCE (HOPKINSVILLE)

Edgar Cayce is considered by many people to be America's greatest twentieth-century prophet. Because of the accuracy of many of his prophecies, he has been compared to Nostradamus. Cayce was born on March 8, 1877, seven miles south of Hopkinsville. The first thirty-five years of his life were spent in Kentucky. He started attending school behind Liberty Christian Church at the age of six. He was formally inducted into Liberty Christian Church in 1888. In 1889, Cayce had his first vision. He was sitting in his hut in the woods when an angel appeared to him and asked him what he wanted. He told her that he wanted to help people, especially sick children. She told him that his prayers were answered.

Cayce attended Liberty Christian Church from 1889 to 1893, when his family moved to Hopkinsville. His psychic abilities began to emerge in 1893, when he was in the eighth grade. He dropped out of the ninth grade, because his parents believed that a ninth-grade education was sufficient for anyone. He started working at Richards Dry Goods Store and Hopper's Book Store at the age of seventeen. He became engaged to Gertrude Evans on March 14, 1897. After working in Louisville for six months, Casey returned to Hopkinsville in December 1899. The next year, Cayce and his father, L.B. Cayce, began selling Woodmen of the World Insurance together.

In 1890, Cayce mysteriously lost his voice. He was able to find a cure for his condition through self-hypnosis. During his sessions, Cayce lay down with his eyes closed and slipped into a trance, during which he verbalized the patients' ailment and recommended a cure. Usually, a stenographer recorded his voice during these sessions and typed up his words. Thousands of these transcripts over a period of twenty-five years have been preserved.

In 1902, Cayce found work as a photographer in Bowling Green. A year after his marriage to Gertrude Evans on June 17, 1903, he opened a photography studio with Frank J. Potter. However, in 1906, their Bowling Green studio was destroyed by fire. On March 16, 1907, Gertrude gave birth to a son, Hugh Lynn Cayce. The joy Edgar felt over being a father was diminished by a fire that destroyed his new photography studio on State Street in September of the same year. By 1909, he had become debt free. In 1910, Edgar began working as a photographer for Russell Brothers studio in Aniston, Alabama. On October 9, 1910, Cayce returned to Hopkinsville, where he and Dr. Wesley Ketchum founded the Psychic Reading Corporation. Under his contract, Cayce agreed to give readings for no money in exchange for use of a photography studio, where he could earn his living.

Edgar Cayce opened a photography studio in Selma, Alabama.

When Cayce discovered that Ketchum was using Cayce's readings for investment purposes, Edgar quit the company. In 1912, he opened a photography studio in Selma, Alabama. On February 9, 1918, Gertrude gave birth to another son, Edgar Evans Cayce. To help make ends meet, Cayce invented a card game, Pit, which was based on the Chicago Board of Trade. By this time, the publicity Cayce was receiving from newspapers attracted the attention of investors and gamblers, who asked for his help in making their fortunes.

In 1923, Cayce and his family moved to Dayton, Ohio. For the next two years, he offered readings for people with health problems. His methods involved the use of electrotherapy, ultraviolet light and gemstones. In 1925, Cayce was in a trance when a voice instructed him to move to Virginia Beach, Virginia, where the crystals in the sand could be used for healing purposes. The period when he lived and worked at Virginia Beach was the most productive of his career. Cayce was supported financially by Morton Blumenthal, who worked in the New York Stock Exchange. He even bought Cayce and his wife a house in Virginia Beach. With the help of the Association of National Investigations, Cayce founded the Cayce Hospital, which was dedicated on October 11, 1928. In this large facility, which contained a lecture hall, offices for researchers and a vault where transcriptions of his readings were stored, Casey and his assistants checked and rechecked his remedies. Cayce's overriding goal was to make his remedies available to the medical profession someday.

During the 1930s, Cayce switched his attention to spirituality. He formed a nonprofit organization called the Association for Research and Enlightenment (ARE). Membership in the organization, which came primarily from Protestant churches, averaged between five hundred and six hundred members by 1940. Between June 1943 and June 1944, Cayce gave 1,385 readings. In August 1944, Cayce collapsed from exhaustion. He and Gertrude moved to the mountains for his health, but he suffered a stroke in September 1944. Cayce died on January 3, 1945. Gertrude outlived him by only three months.

Edgar Cayce is remembered today as the "Sleeping Prophet" as well as the father of holistic medicine. During his lifetime, he gave over fourteen thousand readings. He gained worldwide fame for his predictions, which included World War I, World War II and the Stock Market Crash of 1929. The names on his client list range from ordinary people to luminaries such as Woodrow Wilson, George Gershwin and Thomas Edison. Cayce's legacy continues to this day with the work being conducted by the Edgar Cayce Association for Research and Enlightenment.

Chapter 5

LEGENDARY LOCATIONS

THE JAILER'S INN (BARDSTOWN)

The Jailer's Inn was constructed in a couple of stages. The "Old Jail" was built in 1819 by architect John Rogers on the site of the first jail, which had served the community since 1797. The granite walls are thirty inches thick. Prisoners were housed in two cells and an upstairs dungeon. The back jail, built in 1874, is enclosed by a stone wall. At this time, the Old Jail became the jailer's private residence. The jail closed in 1987 and was converted into a bed-and-breakfast, the Jailer's Inn.

The high levels of paranormal activity reported by guests and employees have been generated, at least in part, by the hundreds of violent criminals who were incarcerated there for almost two hundred years. Crying sounds, piercing screams, disembodied footsteps and the slamming of cell doors have disturbed the sleep of countless guests over the years. One guest was sleeping when someone touched her shoulder and whispered, "Hello," in her ear. A male guest had just unlocked the door to his room when he saw a little girl in an orange dress run across the doorway. A man who was photographing the exterior of the jail captured the image of several ghostly faces in one of the windows. During a visit to the inn, a group of paranormal investigators photographed several orbs in one of the cells.

The courtyard of the Jailer's Inn is haunted as well, mainly because a number of prisoners were hanged there. Many guests have had the uneasy feeling that they were being watched in the courtyard. A male guest may have encountered the ghost of one of the executed prisoners. He said

Built in 1819, Jailer's Inn is now a bed-and-breakfast. Ghosts have been heard crying and screaming in the night.

that, one day, he started up a conversation with a man in the courtyard. The guest looked away for a couple of moments while the other man was speaking. When the guest looked back in the man's direction, he was gone. He believed the ghost may have been one of the inmates of the old jail who has never been released.

THE BODLEY-BULLOCK HOUSE (LEXINGTON)

Originally built for Mayor Thomas Pindell in the Federal style, the Bodley-Bullock House became a hybrid of Greek Revival and Victorian elements. Over the years, a Palladian window above the front door was removed, and a two-story columned portico was added. Later owners also added a two-story columned portico to the side of the house. During the Civil War, the Confederate and Union armies commandeered the house as their headquarters. Afterward, the house passed through a succession of owners before it was purchased by Dr. Waller Bullock in 1912. He went on to establish the Lexington Clinic, and his wife, Minnie, founded the Garden Club of Lexington. After she died in 1970, the Junior League of Lexington leased the house for one dollar a year. After renovating the house, the Junior League used it as its headquarters. The Bodley-Bullock House has become a popular venue for weddings and private parties. It is also a stop on the local ghost tours.

Unlike many antebellum homes, whose ghosts have been generated by their Civil War pasts, the apparition that haunts the Bodley-Bullock House is the spirit of a gardener, Minnie Bullock. Her hatred of alcohol was well known in the community. Supposedly, her husband mocked her temperance beliefs by hanging a portrait of the "town drunk" in the home. The story goes that Mrs. Bullock's will stipulated that no alcohol was to be consumed in her home, but the provision was removed following her death. She expresses her displeasure by cracking tables and flickering lights. During one wedding reception at the house, a photographer captured the image of a woman and a child standing behind the bride on the staircase.

KENTUCKY STATE PENITENTIARY (EDDYVILLE)

In 1884, the Kentucky legislature voted to build the Kentucky State Branch Penitentiary at Eddyville on a hill overlooking the Cumberland River for a cost of $470.753.41. In 1909, prisoners traded in their black-and-white-striped uniforms for baggy denim pants, jackets, cotton shirts and cloth hats. The next year, the electric chair was installed in the penitentiary. Newspaper reports from 1928–29 reveal that approximately fifty men were executed at the prison. Probation began in the 1930s to reduce the surplus population of the prison. Nevertheless, the number of inmates swelled to over one thousand in the 1940s. By the 1950s, the method of execution was changed to lethal injection. A record for the state of Kentucky was set in 1929 when four White prisoners and three Black prisoners were executed on a single night. In 1997, forty-four-year-old Harold McQueen became the first man to be executed in the prison in nearly thirty years. The most recent execution at Kentucky State Penitentiary—November 21, 2008—was of Marco Allen Chapman, who had killed two children six years earlier. A hunger strike took the life of James Kenneth Embry

Jr. in 2014. According to the testimony of inmates and prison guards, the "Castle on the Cumberland," as the prison is called in Eddyville, holds more than living inmates and unpleasant memories.

Some of the most chilling ghost stories from Kentucky's oldest prison come from former corrections officers. Steve Asher, who has written a book about the old prison, *Hauntings of the Kentucky State Penitentiary*, said that he frequently heard screaming and the disembodied voice of someone standing at the gate. While he was working midnights, he saw a shadowy figure walking down the hallway toward him. He also saw a spectral figure standing in the shower. One night, while he was doing his rounds, he heard a scream. He turned on his flashlight, but no one was there. He also saw the image of an inmate wearing black-and-white stripes dating to the turn of the century. In his book, Asher tells the story of a guard in the 1980s who, passing a cell in Three Cell House, saw a man reading a Bible. The prisoner nodded as the guard walked off. Afterward, his sergeant informed the guard that the cell had been empty for quite some time.

Another corrections officer recalled seeing ghosts in the towers and shadowy figures that followed him at midnight while he was making his rounds. One night, he was walking past the unmanned guard tower that houses the controls for the gate to Prison Industries, and the gate opened by itself. This happened so many times after midnight that he and the man who was working with him decided to place a chain lock on the gate. For some of the inmates at Kentucky State Penitentiary, their life sentence has been extended into eternity.

What Is Under Kentucky Lake? (Livingston, Lyon, Trigg, Marshall and Calloway Counties)

Man-made lakes are tailor-made for buried secrets. For example, after the creation of Hoover Dam, Lake Meade was created by flooding several towns, including St. Thomas, which was fifty miles northeast of Las Vegas. Vestiges of this Mormon outpost, such as an old school and an ice-cream parlor, reemerge during periods of drought. In Indiana, the creation of the Salamonie Reservoir completely submerged Monument City. The remains of the brick foundations of houses and the old schools also reappear during droughts. Another of these phantom lake towns lies at the bottom of Kentucky Lake.

The town of Birmingham was established on land owned by Thomas A. Grubbs in 1849. It was named after Birmingham, England, because the founders had hopes of turning it into an iron-smelting town. Remnants of the town's iron foundry still exist in the Land between the Lakes. After the Civil War, the town's prosperity was due largely to its timber industry, which employed approximately 200 people. By 1874, Birmingham had a population of 322, larger than that of the county seat, Benton. In 1894, Birmingham was a thriving town with three grocers, two millinery shops, five churches, two hotels, two schools, a drugstore and two blacksmith shops. In 1908, Birmingham drove out much of its African American population by passing a sundown law. The year 1938 marked the beginning of the end of Birmingham, when the Tennessee Valley Authority (TVA) announced its plans to build the Kentucky Dam and create Kentucky Lake. Residents were told that they would have to move. The TVA began buying up the land in 1942. When the dam was completed in 1944 and the area was flooded, Kentucky Lake became the largest man-made lake in the world at the time, extending 784 miles south across the western tip of Kentucky after Lake Barley was created in the 1960s. Some of the displaced residents of Birmingham had to move again. Today, the remains of streets, access roads and foundations can be seen at Birmingham Point in Kentucky Lake when the water levels are low.

Nevertheless, many of the people who swim, boat or fish on Kentucky Lake are probably unaware that the remnants of an entire town lie under the surface of the water. Only historical records and the memories of elderly residents of Birmingham are keeping the town from fading away. One former resident of Birmingham is eighty-nine-year-old Jackie Bohannon, who was sixteen when she and her family were forced to evacuate. "For my mom and my dad, that was their home. They had been there all their life." George Locker holds an annual reunion for the few surviving residents of Birmingham in memory of his father. After everyone who has some memory of Birmingham passes away, the town will survive primarily in the stories locals tell one another about Kentucky's underwater town.

THE WITCHES' TREE (OLD LOUISVILLE)

Old Louisville in the central part of the city is the third-largest historic district in the United States. Most of the houses lining the streets were built in the Victorian architectural style. The neighborhood also boasts the

The Witches' Tree in Louisville's Historic District is covered with necklaces, occult symbols and charms.

largest number of privately owned homes with stained-glass windows in the country. Other attractions include the Speed Art Museum, a variety of art museums and the Witches' Tree.

The story goes that in the late nineteenth century, a coven of witches used a large tree at Sixth Street and Park Avenue as a meeting place. The witches' nocturnal rituals were tolerated until 1889, when the planning committee decided to cut the tree down and use it as a maypole. Just prior to the tree's removal, the witches vowed that Old Louisville would face very hard times if the tree was cut down. Their prediction turned out to be correct. On March 27, 1890, a devastating tornado destroyed churches, businesses and the train station. The cause of the storm became readily apparent to the more superstitious members of the community when a sapling started growing in place of the tree. As the new tree matured, locals were appalled by its gnarled and twisted appearance. Today, the limbs and branches of the Witches' Tree are covered with necklaces, occult symbols and charms, such as a horseshoe, which some people believe acts as an anti-witch totem. Some of these tributes may have been left by tourists and people in the community who feel it is best to err on the side of caution. Not surprisingly, the Witches' Tree has become a popular stop on local ghost tours.

LIBERTY HALL (FRANKFORT)

John Brown (1757–1837) is one of Kentucky's most revered founding fathers. This pioneering lawmaker distinguished himself early on as an aide to the Marquis de Lafayette and as a member of the Continental Congress. When he began construction of his mansion on a four-acre estate in Frankfort in 1796, he used architectural plans drawn up by Thomas Jefferson, under whom Brown had studied law. He named his home Liberty Hall after his alma mater, the Virginia Academy. The house was built with bricks fired on-site and with hardwood rafters and flooring. Brown's wife oversaw the design of the interior, furnishing her new home with brass door handles and locks, mirrors, window glass and antiques from Europe. Liberty Hall soon became the showplace of Frankfort, where the Browns entertained luminaries such as President James Monroe, Colonel Andrew Jackson, Colonel Zachary Taylor, Aaron Burr and General Lafayette. Brown's descendants continued to occupy Liberty Hall until 1937, when the home and many of the original furnishings were willed to Liberty Hall Inc. Since 1956, Liberty Hall has been managed by the National Society of the Colonial Dames of America. Over time, Liberty Hall gained a reputation as one of its most historic—and most haunted—homes.

Several ghosts are believed to haunt Liberty Hall. One of them is the spirit of an opera singer from Spain who performed in Frankfort. Following the concert, the Browns invited her to stay at Liberty Hall. In the middle of a reception given in her honor, she walked down the garden path to the Kentucky River. She was never seen again. Some people say her terror-stricken specter runs through the garden on hot summer nights. A second apparition that has been sighted at Liberty Hall is the ghost of a soldier wearing a British uniform from the War of 1812. He usually appears looking through a window into the living room.

The most famous ghost is undoubtedly the spirit of Mrs. Brown's aunt, Margaret Varick, who had taken custody of the girl after her mother's death. When one of Mrs. Brown's children took ill, her family urged Varick to come to Liberty Hall. The rigors of the journey by coach and horseback took their toll on the elderly lady, who died of exhaustion. The bereaved family buried Brown's aunt in the family plot, but the grave site was lost after the family's graves were moved to a larger cemetery in Frankfort. Mrs. Varick's ghost became active not long after the family plot was relocated. Wearing a gray housedress, Brown's kindly aunt has been sighted in every room at Liberty Hall. The bride of John Brown's grandson Benjamin was the first to witness the "Gray Lady" in Liberty Hall while spending the night in Mrs. Varrick's former bedroom. The horrified young woman swore that she saw the Gray Lady walk across the bedroom floor. A visitor named Rebecca Averill saw the Gray Lady standing in front of the fireplace. Rebecca was so frightened that she pulled the covers over her head. A few minutes later, the ghost was gone. Benjamin Gatz Brown's niece said she saw the Gray Lady standing by her bed. A college professor came to Liberty Hall to investigate reports of the Gray Lady standing in front of a window. He said he was awakened one night by the touch of cold fingers on his cheek. When he opened his eyes, he was shocked to see the Gray Lady smiling down at him. A curator who took several photographs inside the house captured the image of a woman descending the staircase. A docent who lived in an upstairs apartment claimed that the Gray Lady shut the bathroom door to give her privacy while she was taking a bath. The docent also credited Mrs. Varick's ghost with turning on a music box while she was reminiscing about an old boyfriend. The Gray Lady, it seems, has the ability to instill fear in some eyewitnesses and gratitude in others.

Bobby Mackey's Music World (Wilder)

The building in which Bobby Mackey's Music World is housed was erected in 1850 as a slaughterhouse, which supplied meat products. The lowest level of the building was used to store blood and offal. Evidence suggests that after the slaughterhouse closed in the 1890s, satanists congregated and performed their ceremonies around the well and may have sacrificed animals here for their covert rituals. The infamous incident in the building's history occurred in 1896. An unmarried twenty-two-year-old woman named Pearl Bryant arrived in Cincinnati so that her boyfriend, a dental student named Scott Jackson, could set up an abortion. Instead of Bryant being taken to a physician, Jackson and his roommate, Alonzo M. Walling, tried to perform the operation themselves, and she died as a result of their lack of training. According to some contemporary accounts, Pearl was still alive when Jackson and Walling cut off her head. They covered up their crime by hiding her head and her body in two separate locations. The men dumped Pearl's body in a field; her head, however, has never been found. Nevertheless, the authorities were able to identify the body by the custom-made shoes that Jackson and Walling had neglected to remove from her feet. The fate of Pearl's head has become the stuff of legend. Many locals believe that Jackson decapitated Pearl so that her head could be used by a satanic cult he belonged to. Another legend has it that while Walling was waiting to be hanged, he promised to haunt the old slaughterhouse forever.

The slaughterhouse's violent legacy continued, even after it was razed at the beginning of the twentieth century. In the 1920s, a speakeasy/casino was built on the site. In the 1930s, E.A. "Buck" Brady purchased the casino and renamed it the Primrose. Ten years later, when gangsters from Cincinnati attempted to take over the operation, Buck decided to close the casino in 1946. In the 1950s, the Cleveland Syndicate converted the former casino into a nightclub called the Latin Quarter. The story goes that a dance-hall girl named Johanna, who was also the daughter of the owner, fell in love with a singer named Robert Randall. After becoming pregnant, she decided to run off with her lover. However, her father learned of her plans and hired a mobster to have him killed. His daughter was so distraught by the news of Randall's death that her mind became unhinged. She poisoned her father and then killed herself in the basement.

Violence became a trademark of the nightclub for the next couple of decades. In 1978, a country music singer named Bobby Mackey bought the building and transformed it into Bobby Mackey's Music World. He had previously earned a living working on farms and railroads; as the owner of a nightclub, he now had an opportunity to indulge his passion for music. Owing to more than forty reports of paranormal activity, the roadhouse has gained a reputation as the most haunted nightclub in the United States. One of the earliest tales dates to the 1990s, when a car speeding down Licking Road struck a telephone pole outside of Bobby Mackey's Music World. All of the occupants of the car were killed instantly. The first policeman on the scene, Larry Hornsby, was examining the damage to the car when a woman came out of the nightclub and offered him a couple of tablecloths to place over the faces of the victims. When he returned the next week to thank her, he was surprised that no woman matching her description had been in the building that night.

Patrons and employees have contributed their personal experiences with the paranormal to the growing body of ghost legends. One customer reported feeling intense cold in certain spots and seeing a trash can fly across the room. When he was in the men's restroom, the same guest claimed to have seen the apparition of a man with a handlebar moustache repeating over and over again the Latin expression *die game*, which means "dying well." People have seen a headless ghost dressed in late nineteenth-century clothing inside the building. Bobby Mackey's wife had a number of supernatural encounters in the basement, including detecting the scent of roses. She was also attacked by a figure that grabbed her around the waist, picked her up and threw her down. It also pushed her down the stairs and screamed, "Get out!" Afterward, she realized that the face of her assailant resembled that of Alonzo Walling, drawings of whom she had seen in the past. An exorcism was held inside Bobby Mackey's Music World for a caretaker who believed that he was possessed by an evil spirit. A former manager said that on several occasions, she locked up the venue for the night, only to find a short time later that the lights were turned on and the jukebox was playing "The Anniversary Waltz," despite being unplugged at the time.

Paranormal investigators have suggested that because ghosts are believed to be incapable of crossing flowing water, the nightclub's proximity to the Licking River has prevented the spirits from crossing to the other side. Over the years, Bobby Mackey has made the most of his nightclub's ghostly occurrences. Patrons can purchase a variety of T-shirts, books and other souvenirs to commemorate their visit to what many have called the "Portal of Hell." Ghosts, combined with music and entertainment, are definitely big business.

CAMP ZACHARY TAYLOR (LOUISVILLE)

Camp Taylor was the largest of sixteen World War I army training camps in the United States. Built in 1917 on two thousand acres of farmland, it was located near a sixteen-thousand-acre artillery range dating to the Civil War. The camp itself was named after General Zachary Taylor, while the streets bore the names of generals like William Tecumseh Sherman and Robert E. Lee. Soldiers stationed there wrote home about the camp's hot meals, laundry service and comfortable accommodations. The camp was fortified against any kind of assault except for airborne disease. The 1918 influenza epidemic decimated Camp Zachary Taylor, largely because so many men were living in close quarters. The first case was reported in September 1918. In just a few weeks, over one thousand soldiers succumbed to the disease. For a while, sixty-nine men were dying each day. Because of the lack of morgue space, bodies were piled on top of one another from floor to ceiling in several of the buildings. According to local lore, many of the bodies were removed from the camp at night to prevent panic from sweeping through Louisville.

Most of Camp Taylor was dismantled three years after it was founded. In 1921, fifteen hundred parcels of land were auctioned off, and a residential neighborhood rose on the site of the former training camp. Keith Age, the director of the Louisville Ghost Hunters Society, said that much of the lumber from the military buildings was used in construction of the homes. The psychic residue remaining on the boards may be responsible for the high levels of paranormal activity reported in the neighborhood. Ken Maguire, founder and curator of the Camp Zachary Taylor Historical Society, said, "I've heard people talk about paranormal activity in the hospital area, which was along Durrett Lane and Preston." The apparition of a woman wearing a blue Victorian-era dress has been seen walking along the streets. The ghosts of women from nearby bordellos have been sighted as well. Many people living in the neighborhood have heard the spectral tones of a bugle early in the morning. Ghostly soldiers, marching in formation, occasionally appear across the streets and fields

Only a few remnants of Fort Zachary Taylor are still visible. Consequently, few of the people who live in houses erected on the site of the former training grounds are even aware of its existence. Memories of the camp are manifested in the occasional spirits that announce their presence by disrupting the tranquility of the neighborhoods.

THE BROWN HOTEL (LOUISVILLE)

Early in 1923, businessman J. Graham Brown began construction of the hotel that bears his name at the corner of Fourth and Broadway, which was an established promenade in Louisville. Completed at a cost of $4 million, the sixteen-story hotel opened ten months later, on October 25, 1923. The exterior was designed in the Georgian style; the interior design reflects the English Renaissance style. Guests reveled in the hotel's crystal chandeliers, Palladian windows, Botticino limestone floors and hand-painted coffered ceilings. The Brown Hotel energized the growing downtown area. Two years later, Brown erected the Brown Office Building nearby. In the 1920s, hundreds of people attended dinner dances at the Brown Hotel. The Brown Hotel's fortunes waned in the 1930s. Because he defaulted on a loan, Brown had to ask his employees to work without pay for a short while. When the Ohio River flooded the downtown area, including the Brown Hotel, the kitchen staff fed the thousand-plus people who had sought refuge in the six hundred guest rooms. Buckets of water were carried up fifteen flights of stairs so that the toilets would flush. Business improved immensely during World War II; soldiers waited in line for hours to get a room. Over the years, a number of celebrities have stayed at the Brown Hotel during the week of the Kentucky Derby, the city's most important annual social holiday. Famous guests who took advantage of the hotel's lavish accommodations included Harry Truman, Elizabeth Taylor, the Duke of Windsor, Robert Young, Joan Crawford, Muhammad Ali, Jimmy Carter, George H.W. Bush and Barack Obama. Business dropped off drastically after Brown's death in 1969, leading to the hotel's closure in 1971. For a while, it housed the Jefferson County Public School's board of education. Since the 1980s, the Brown Hotel has passed through a variety of hotel chains before being purchased and renovated by 1859 Historic Hotels in 2006.

The hauntings at the Brown Hotel began soon after renovations commenced in 2006, leading to speculation that the improvements "stirred up" the spirits. The hotel is said to be haunted by the ghost of J. Graham Brown, who lived on the fifteenth floor in the penthouse. The fifteenth floor is used only for storage space, but staff who have ventured up there have reported seeing footprints in the dust. Guests and staff say that the elevator occasionally stops at the fifteenth floor for no apparent reason. Guests saying on the fourth floor have complained about being awakened by the sound of heavy furniture being moved on the floor above them. Hotel staff have heard whispers, groans and weird noses throughout the hotel. Cold spots

Left: J. Graham Brown built the Brown Hotel in 1923 at the corner of Fourth and Broadway Streets.

Below: This statue is made in the likeness of J. Graham Brown, whose ghost haunts the second-floor mezzanine in April during Derby Week.

appear in the hotel in random places in the hot summer months. Orbs have been seen in the fireplaces when no fires are burning. The distinctive odor of cigars drifts through the hotel occasionally, even though no smoking is allowed on the premises. Brown's apparition has been sighted on the second-floor mezzanine in April during Kentucky Derby Week so that he can keep an eye on guests and employees. Eyewitnesses describe him as a man in an old-style tuxedo. People who approached the ghostly figure say that it tends to dissipate as it walks around a lobby column or a corner. Brown's ghost, it seems, is still micromanaging the hotel that was his home and his place of business for so many years.

THE L&N RAILROAD TRACKS (LaGRANGE)

The Louisville Railroad was chartered by the Commonwealth of Kentucky in 1850. Its 180-mile expansion to Nashville took place in 1859. After the outbreak of the Civil War, the L&N Railroad benefited greatly from its huge haulage contracts with the Union army for the transport of troops and supplies. In the early 1900s, the L&N Railroad was able to expand into the coal-rich terrain of Kentucky because its steam locomotives burned coal. During World War II, the L&N experienced an 80 percent increase in freight traffic because of the high demand for the transportation of munitions and supplies. One of the towns that prospered after the arrival of the L&N was LaGrange. The LaGrange Railroad Museum at 412 Main Street is housed in the old 1910 Train Depot, where visitors can view railroad memorabilia and large model train sets. The railroad tracks, which run alongside downtown Main Street, are also the site of some terrifying ghost stories.

The Oldham County History Center at LaGrange is the source of one of the country's many tragic railroad ghost stories. In 1955, a young girl named Mary Westerfield took a shortcut along the railroad tracks just outside the city limits. Without the benefit of moonlight or a flashlight, she had to make her way back to town in almost pitch darkness. For some unknown reason, she did not see or hear the speeding locomotive that struck her, killing her instantly. Some locals speculated at the time that she might have stepped in front of the train to commit suicide. To this day, people say that anyone passing by the tracks just outside of town at night can hear the residual screams of Mary Westerfield as she was run over by the train.

This L&N express car and hundreds of railroad cars like it were a common sight throughout the South between 1850 and 1982. *Courtesy of Wikimedia Commons.*

Only three blocks away from the LaGrange Railroad Museum is the Rails Restaurant at 117 Main Street. This 150-year-old building has housed two restaurants: the Irish Rover Too Restaurant and, most recently, the Rails Restaurant. It is believed to be haunted by the ghost of an eight-year-old girl known only as Jennie, who died from typhoid fever in the late 1800s. For years, the apparition of a little girl wearing a white dress and a white hair bow has been seen walking around the parking lot and behind the restaurant. She is a mischievous spirit who torments members of the staff by touching them on the arm and moving dishes to other spots during the night. Employees who open up the restaurant in the morning have been surprised to find that the chairs that had been placed on the tables the night before were now on the floor. Childish laughter has been heard throughout the old building. While the Rails was being remodeled, workers who arrived in the morning were puzzled to find that several toys had been placed out of the reach of children. Most employees agree, though, that an occasional inconvenience is a small price to pay for the presence of such a playful little ghost.

THE MANDY TREE (MADISONVILLE)

Stories of haunted trees can be found throughout the United States. Standing in a field in Somerset County, New Jersey, is the Devil's Tree, which is said to curse anyone who tries to damage it. In Needham, Alabama, strange cries coming from a pecan tree drew hundreds of people to Linnie Jenkins's front yard in April 1981. Kentucky has two haunted trees. One of them is the gnarled and twisted Witch Tree in Louisville. The other is the Mandy Tree in Madisonville.

Author Byron Crawford recounts the story of the Mandy Tree in an article that appeared in *Kentucky Living* on October 1, 2016. Like many legends, Mandy Holloman's sad ending is based on fact. According to Maggie Bowman, a member of the Historical Society of Hopkins County, the nude body of a young African American woman was discovered by her children in 1915. The body was wrapped in a quilt blanket near a white oak tree that she had planted herself. The authorities determined that she had been shot and declared her death a suicide. Because Mandy was such a loving wife and mother, her family and friends could not fathom why anyone would want to kill her, but they were convinced that someone had.

Mandy's former home was eventually purchased by African Methodist ministers H.V. and Madeline C. Taylor. Mrs. Taylor first noticed the resemblance of the foliage of the white oak tree to Mandy Holloman after she prayed to the Lord to prevent the bank from taking her beloved home. Mrs. Taylor told her grandson that she could clearly make out the shape of Mandy Bowman's face and even the collar of her dress in the leaves. Before long, word spread throughout the community about the strange tree in the Taylors' yard. Mrs. Taylor made enough money by selling refreshments to the throngs of sightseers to help pay her mortgage. Within a few months, the story was published in *Ripley's Believe or Not!* and *Life Magazine*. The tree stood for several decades before finally being destroyed by lightning. One of the photographs taken of the tree was sold to a private collector in the 1970s.

In an interesting postscript to the legend, a worker made a fascinating discovery while he was remodeling Mandy Holloman's former home. Inside a wall near the fireplace, he found a rifle. The gun was given to Mandy Holloman's great-nephew John T. Taylor.

THE GRATZ PARK INN (LEXINGTON)

The two-story building that houses the Gratz Park Inn was constructed in 1916 as an office complex for three doctors: Waller O. Bullock, David Woolfold Barrow and David Barrow. The Franklin and Curtis architectural firm designed the building in the Colonial Revival style. By 1920, the three doctors' joint practice had increased to nine doctors. To accommodate the increased size of the office, several rooms were added, one of the wings was enlarged and the name was changed to the Lexington Clinic. According to legend, a bootlegger went to the clinic to have a stick removed from his eye. Supposedly, the stick had been lodged in his eye socket fifteen years before when he was trying to evade a whiskey revenuer. The building housed the Fuller Engineering firm from 1958 until 1976. The vacant building was renovated in 1987, when it was converted into the Gratz Park Inn. Today, the luxury hotel offers guests a taste of the past with its four-posted beds, antique furniture and ghosts.

According to employees, three ghosts haunt the Gratz Park Inn. One is the spirit of a little girl who has been christened "Lizzie" by the staff. She is a playful ghost who tugs on the sleeves of guests, plays jacks and dolls on the third floor and opens and closes doors. She is probably the ghostly child whose running in the hallways has awakened guests. Another ghost is the spirit of John, an African American man in a plaid shirt who cradles his face in his hands. Historical records indicate that he may have been the first patient treated at the clinic, possibly from a gunshot wound. Little is known about the third apparition, the "Lady in White," who has been seen throughout the hotel. Eyewitnesses get the impression from her face that she is looking for somebody. The hotel's high level of spirit activity might stem from the remnants of the old clinic that can still be found there, such as the scuppers in the basement morgue.

BUFFALO TRACE DISTILLERY (FRANKFORT)

Buffalo Trace Distillery has the reputation of being the oldest continually operating distillery in the United States. Hankcock Lee and his brother Willis Lee began distilling whiskey on the present-day site of the Buffalo Trace Distillery in 1765. Harrison Blanton built a distillery here in 1812. In 1869, Edmund H. Taylor bought the distillery and renamed it the Old Fire

Copper (OFC) Brewery. He tore down the distillery and replaced it with a larger one in 1873. When lightning destroyed the facility in 1882, Taylor rebuilt it on top of the previous building. By the end of the year, the OFC Brewery was back in business. In 1886, Taylor sold the brewery. In 1886, the new owner, George T. Stagg, created climate-controlled warehouses by installing steam heating. During Prohibition (1920–33), the president of the Buffalo Trace Distillery, Colonel Albert B. Blanton, was able to keep it open by producing medicinal-quality whiskey. While one of the buildings was being remodeled in October 2016, the foundation of the original 1873 building was uncovered. According to legend, the spirits of some of the men who were instrumental in building and operating the Buffalo Trace Distillery still make their presence known.

According to an article that appeared in the October 1, 2017 edition of *Kentucky Monthly*, the Buffalo Trace Distillery is haunted by several ghosts. Ironically, two of the most frequently sighted ghosts in the brewery are the spirits of two little girls. One of the little girls lingers around the visitors' center. A group of painters were working inside the center after hours when they saw a little girl wearing an old-fashioned dress standing in a corner of a room on the second floor. She vanished in a matter of seconds. A few months later, a tour guide in the brewery said that one day he arrived at the visitors' center to get a room on the second floor ready for a wedding. As he pulled up to the building, he was surprised to find that all of the lights were on in one of the rooms on the second floor. He immediately became apprehensive when he recalled that the lights were activated by motion sensors. He became even more anxious on discovering that all of the doors were locked. After a security guard let him in, he heard footsteps coming from the second floor. To kill time while waiting for his crew to arrive, the tour guide began straightening up on the first floor when he heard noises coming from a bar on the other side of the wall. When he peeked around the corner, he was shocked to find that no one was there. His fear gradually waned when it occurred to him that the troublesome ghost was possibly the spirit of a child who was having fun at his expense. The apparition of a second girl has been photographed standing in front of a tree near the Blanton Mansion. Possible candidates for the identity of the ghosts are two little girls who lived across the street from the distillery. One of them perished after falling into a well; the other one succumbed to yellow fever.

One of the male ghosts haunting the building is thought to be the vigilant spirit of Colonel Edmund Taylor. His spirit has appeared throughout the distillery. His best-known appearance took place in the old Warehouse C, built in 1885. The story goes that the foreman of a work crew was taking a short nap when he heard a disembodied voice saying, "Get your men out of the way." Thinking that he was dreaming, the man fell into a deep slumber. A few minutes later, he was awakened once again by someone whispering, "Get the men out of here!" The foreman jumped to his feet and ordered his men to evacuate the building. They had no sooner left the warehouse than one of the brick walls collapsed at the place where they had been working. Like Colonel Taylor, the specter was looking out for the welfare of the workers.

Colonel Taylor's penchant for micromanagement was revealed in a different building—Warehouse D—during a guided tour. The guide was speaking to his tour group when he noticed a man wearing khaki pants peering into a barrel and writing on a clipboard. The guide assumed that the man was a tourist who had wandered off, so he asked him to rejoin the group. Ignoring the tour guide's request, the strange figure walked straight into a barrel and vanished.

The personal experiences of some of the staff suggest that spirits of other employees are still on the job as well. Employees and visitors have reported hearing ghostly voices coming from Albert Blanton's former meeting room. A security guard taking a walk-through of the distillery late one night investigated the lights that were on inside the gift shop. He opened the door, expecting to find someone there, but the shop was empty. The Buffalo Trace Distillery, it seems, is a busy place, even when no one is there.

The Land between the Lakes National Recreation Area (Golden Pond)

The Land between the Lakes National Recreation Area (LBL) comprises 170,000 acres of wetlands, fields and forests. Over 1.5 million people visit LBL annually for its hiking and biking trails, water trails, abundance of wildlife and opportunities for hunting and fishing. Many people camp here in the hope of seeing some of the beaver, bison and elk in the park, as well as egrets, osprey and maybe an eagle or two. Others come to LBL to explore the truth behind the park's various legends.

One of these creepy places has been christened the "Vampire Hotel" by the teenagers who partied there in the 1990s. This dilapidated structure was originally the private residence of Dorothy B. Keith. The one-story

Visitors to the Land between the Lakes State Park have reported seeing a phantom truck, a wolf-like creature and the ghosts of runaway slaves. *Courtesy of Wikimedia Commons.*

house was built sometime after the creation of Kentucky Lake in 1945. At one time, the luxurious vacation home had a walk-out basement adjacent to an arch-shaped patio with a cistern. Part of the stone and concrete house was destroyed in the 1960s. After the house was featured in an episode of the televisions series *Unsolved Mysteries* about a vampire cult in 1996, the rest of the house was razed in 1997 to prevent even more curiosity seekers from flocking to the site. The vampire cult, led by Rod Ferrell, was rumored to have stayed in the house during their murderous rampage in the early 1990s, but no evidence exists that they actually visited LBL at this time. Today, nothing remains of the Vampire Hotel except for part of the patio's semicircular wall, as well as largely apocryphal tales of blood-drinking rituals and animal sacrifice.

A legend with more sinister overtones is the story of the trucker who was killed one night when his truck crashed on Highway 65/80. A number of people claim to have been followed by the phantom truck while driving through LBL after sundown. As a rule, the truck's headlights vanish as the driver leaves the park.

Some of the park's unexplained sights and sounds may also have a supernatural source. One of the two-legged phantoms that has appeared in the more heavily wooded parts of LBL is said to be a creature from Native American lore that has lupine facial features and red eyes. The spirits of runaway slaves who took refuge here in the first half of the nineteenth century have also been sighted in the park. The orbs and mists that visitors have reported seeing in the area could be the result of the flooding of several cemeteries in the 1940s during the creation of Kentucky Lake. Some locals believe that the gunshots and screams that have been heard in the woods around the lake may be the residual sounds of Civil War skirmishes. Clearly, the park's dark side stands in stark contrast with the fun side of LBL.

HELL'S HALF ACRE (PADUCAH)

Like many cities, Paducah once had a number of small neighborhoods, each of which had a reputation of its own, like Lowertown, Uppertown, Little Frenchtown, Jersey City, Arcadia and Mechanicsburg. Some of these "little towns" were viewed by the locals as "dens of iniquity," such as Pistol Avenue, Dogtown, Monkey Wrench Park, Hotsprings and the Bucket of Blood. One of the worst of these shady areas was Hell's Half Acre.

The neighborhood that became known as Hell's Half Acre was located at the corner of Washington and South Second. It was originally settled by George Wyatt, who was given the land by his brother Charles. In 1860, the Wyatts sold the land to John Lynn, who operated a small grocery store and boardinghouse. A tobacco factory was built on the property as well. By 1861, the area around Lynn's house had become so disreputable that even the police refused to venture there. After the Civil War, the area became known for its gambling dens and bars. The baseball diamond and racetrack built on the land attracted even more gamblers, as well as "painted ladies" and an assortment of rowdies. One of the most infamous denizens of Hell's Half Acre was Nut Knox, who lived in a cave and carried an axe. Rumors soon spread that he was behind some of the disappearances in the area. Hell's Half Acre began to erode after the arrival of the railroad in the late 1880s. The land was absorbed by the Southern Hotel and, later on, by the Iseman Wagon Yard. Little remains of Hell's Half Acre except for remnants of the tobacco factory and the graveyard.

Not surprisingly, Hell's Half Acre has produced a number of legends. According to an article published in the *Messenger* on September 6, 1996, the guerrillas who descended on Hell's Half Acre during the Civil War buried their stolen gold and, possibly, a body under one of the houses that once stood there. A number of people have had brushes with the paranormal there as well. The story goes that as John Lynn lay dying in his bedroom, a redbird perched on the window and chirped like a whip-poor-will. On the day of Lynn's funeral, the same bird lit on his coffin and chirped like a whip-poor-will while the casket was being carried to the grave site. In the early 1900s, a man driving a wagon through Hell's Half Acre was startled by the sudden appearance of a small white dog keeping pace with the wagon. When the man cracked the whip, the dog suddenly appeared on the other side of the wagon. The dog continued running alongside the wagon all the way back home. More recently, a group of hunters was walking through the nearby woods after dark when they heard something running ahead of them. When it exited the trees, the creature jumped on top of their truck and leapt off the other side. Although the men didn't actually see the thing, they were convinced that it was real when they examined the large tracks on top of the truck. The houses, saloons and bordellos that made up the district may be gone, but its infamy lives on in the stories people still tell about Hell's Half Acre.

THE META BAR (LOUISVILLE)

The Meta Cocktail Bar is located at 425 West Chestnut Street. The building in which it is housed was erected in the mid-1800s. Before co-owners Jeremy Johnson and Hannah Kandle opened the bar in 2013, it was home to the Show-n-Tell strip club. From the beginning, Johnson and Kandle envisioned an upscale bar where customers could sample wine, craft beer, "high street food," live music and signature cocktails like its chocolate-and-fig variation of the Old Fashioned called the Never Have I Ever. Part of the high-end bar's appeal is undoubtedly the stories customers and employees still tell about a murder that occurred there in the mid-twentieth century.

After Jeremy Johnson took over the old building, he was surprised to find a large picture of a reclining nude woman in storage. He found out from some of the previous tenants that when the building was used as a strip club, the painting of one of the dancers hung on a wall. The dancer was in

The ghost of a murdered dancer shows its dislike for some of the male patrons of the Meta Bar.

the habit of sitting with her painting between shifts, admiring the way the artist captured her beauty. One day, one of the customers began arguing with the girl and killed her.

The infamous painting is now hanging behind red curtains in the liquor store in the rear of the bar. Judging from the negative encounters some of the customers have had in the bar, Jeremy Johnson has concluded that the spirit of the murdered stripper has an aversion to men "she doesn't like the look of." She expresses her dislike of certain types of men by moving objects like keys to different parts of the building. Both of the co-owners of Meta have experienced feelings of unease in parts of the building, possibly because of the presence of the woman in the painting. Their suspicions that their business is haunted were confirmed when they witnessed a woman dressed in 1960s fashions walk into the back hallway. The screams people have heard coming from the mop closet are particularly unnerving. "I saw this stuff happen," Johnson said. "Call it an energy or whatever you want to call it, but something's going on."

SLEEPY HOLLOW ROAD (LOUISVILLE)

Haunted roads can be found all across the United States. A number of urban legends and ghost stories have grown up around Boy Scout Lane in Steven's Point, Wisconsin, where an entire troop of Boy Scouts were said to have been murdered by the scoutmaster or the bus driver. Riverview Drive in Totowa, New Jersey, is referred to by the locals as "Annie's Drive." According to the legend, Annie was hit and killed by a truck on her prom night in the 1960s. People driving down the road at night claim to hear her disembodied screams. A "mish-mash" beast known as the Pigman has been sighted along Devil's Washburn Road in Moretown, Vermont. Although Sleepy Hollow Road in Louisville, Kentucky, has nothing to do with terrified schoolmasters or headless horsemen, it is still considered one of the most haunted roads in the state.

Not far from the town of Prospect is a winding stretch of two-lane blacktop. At sunset, the arching canopy of trees is transformed into a dark, foreboding tunnel. The guardrail prevents speeding cars from plummeting into the thirty-foot ravine. The shadows of the trees in the moonlight fuel the imagination of lonely drivers as they recall the legends of Sleepy Hollow Road. Driving over the modern-looking concrete bridge brings to mind an old covered bridge that once stood there. Teenagers who came over there to party called it the "Crybaby Bridge" because of the sad tales of desperate mothers who tossed their unwanted infants over the side. Locals say that the wails of the mothers and the cries of the babies can still be heard at the site of the old bridge, echoing in the darkness.

The dangers of driving too fast on Sleepy Hollow Road are probably the inspiration for the story of the phantom trucker. A number of drivers claim to have been pursued by a semi that appears seemingly out of nowhere. As the truck comes closer, the drivers speed up to avoid being rear-ended. The drivers don't realize they are being chased by a hearse until it pulls alongside them and slams into their car, forcing them to crash through the guardrail to their death below. Actually, the presence of a hearse on Sleepy Hollow Road is not implausible, because the road passes Harrod's Creek Cemetery.

An even more sinister area just off Sleepy Hollow Road is Devil's Point. This is the place where, in the 1970s and 1980s, satanists were believed to have performed their dark rites, some of which involved the sacrifice of animals and human beings. The cries of the celebrants' victims resound through trees and hollows. Some brave souls who ventured into the isolated area swore that they saw people in black robes dancing and chanting around their bonfires.

According to a posting by Jay Gravatte of the Louisville Ghost Hunters Society, Sleepy Hollow Road may also be a portal through time. People who have driven onto the road have suddenly found themselves several miles away. "Lost time" is just one of many eerie experiences that have been reported on Sleepy Hollow Road.

THE SEELBACH HOTEL (LOUISVILLE)

The Seelbach Hotel is one of the most famous—maybe even infamous—hotels because of its long and storied past. In the mid-1800s, two brothers from Bavaria, Louis and Otto Seelbach, immigrated to the United States to make their fortune in restaurants and clubs. In 1903, they began construction of a luxury hotel at the corner of Fourth and Walnut Streets. In May 1905, twenty-five thousand people attended the grand opening of the beautiful Beaux-Arts, Baroque hotel. Visitors marveled at the hotel's interior furnishings, including its lobby fashioned from mahogany, bronze and marble and its vaulted dome of two hundred panes.

Over the years, a parade of the rich and famous passed through the doors of the Seelbach Hotel. The list of luminaries includes a number of presidents, such as William Howard Taft, Woodrow Wilson, Franklin Roosevelt, Harry Truman, John F. Kennedy, Jimmy Carter and Bill Clinton. In the 1920s, several gangland figures turned the Seelbach into their private playground. Dutch Schulz and Lucky Luciano spent time there playing cards, relaxing and drinking. Al Capone was undoubtedly the most famous gangster who stayed there. He was said to have dined and played cards in a small alcove in the Oakroom. When F. Scott Fitzgerald visited the Seelbach while stationed at Camp Taylor in 1918, he met an underworld kingpin named George Remus, whom the writer used as inspiration for Jay Gatsby in *The Great Gatsby*. Fitzgerald also modeled the ballroom where Daisy and Tom Buchanan held their wedding after the Seelbach's Grand Ballroom.

Follow the deaths of Louis Seelbach in 1923 and Otto Seelbach in 1933, the Seelbach Hotel passed through several owners, who remodeled it. The hotel closed in 1968 and stood abandoned for ten years before it was renovated by Roger Davis and H.G. Whittenberg Jr. in 1978. The Seelbach reopened to great fanfare in 1982. The Metropolitan Life Insurance Company took

Left: Louis and Otto Seelbach built the Seelbach Hotel at Fourth and Walnut Streets in 1903.

Below: The Seelbach's magnificent lobby was furnished with bronzes from France, wood from the West Indies and Europe and marble from Italy, Germany and France.

Al Capone is said to have played cards with his cronies in the Oakroom.

over the hotel in 1984. After Meristar Hotels and Resorts purchased it in 1998, the new owners turned over the supervision of the Seelbach to Hilton Hotels. Following the hotel's acquisition by Investcorp International in 2007, the hotel was renamed the Seelbach Hilton Louisville. Not only is it listed in the National Register of Historic Places, but it also bears the distinction of being one of the most haunted hotels in Kentucky.

An entity known as the Blue Lady has been walking the halls of the Seelbach Hotel since 1987, when two different people saw a woman in a blue dress walk through the elevator doors on the mezzanine level and the eighth floor. That same year, one of the hotel's chefs looked out of the Oakroom door and caught sight of a woman in a blue chiffon dress with long black hair walk inside the elevator. His eyes widened when he realized that the elevator's doors had not opened. A few minutes later, a maid saw the Blue Lady walk through the elevator's closed doors on the second floor. Curiosity regarding the identity of the ghost drove the staff members to do newspaper research in the archives in the library. After a few hours, they found a newspaper article dating back to 1936 that reported the death of one of the hotel's guests, Patricia Wilson, who moved to Louisville from

The ghost of the Lady in Blue was seen walking through the closed elevator doors on the eighth floor.

Oklahoma. She and her husband had been separated for four years, and they planned to meet at the Seelbach Hotel to talk about getting back together. Not realizing that her estranged husband had been killed in an automobile accident on his way to the hotel, Patricia waited several hours for him in the lobby before walking toward the elevator. On the morning of July 16, 1936, one of the staff members found her body lying on top of a dummy elevator car at the hotel. For many years, people have wondered if she mistakenly entered the dummy elevator, which was used only to transport linens, or if she intentionally plunged down the elevator shaft. Since that first sighting, Patricia Wilson's spirit has manifested on the eighth floor and the mezzanine.

However, the Blue Lady is not the only spirit that is a permanent guest at the hotel. Author Larry Johnson, the lobby concierge at the Seelbach, said that in 1985, a woman called down to the front desk one night, complaining that after she got beneath the covers and turned off the light, she felt something rub against her legs. Johnson reported the appearance of a strange heart-shaped bubble underneath the wallpaper in the same room that resisted all attempts to remove it. Some guests have walked into cold spots in specific areas of the hotel and smelled perfume in unexpected places. The ghost of an elderly woman wearing an old, torn dress has been seen standing behind the mirror in the Otto Café. In 2004, a honeymooning couple was asleep in their room on the eighth floor when, suddenly, the young man was awakened by a sudden drop in temperature. He looked across the room and, in the glow of the streetlight, saw a man standing in front of the window. He was holding the drapes open, as if he was waiting for someone to show up. When the young man turned on the light, the ghostly intruder vanished. The temperature rose back to normal. Larry Johnson, the author of *The Seelbach: A Hilton Hotel*, suggests that the ghost may have been the spirit of Mr. Wilson returned to the Seelbach to meet up with his wife.

THE SAND MOUNTAIN GHOST LIGHTS
(JEFFERSON AND MEANS COUNTIES)

Sand Mountain is a series of towering, rounded hills in the Cumberland Plateau of the Appalachian Mountains. It is located twelve miles south of Mount Sterling between Jeffersonville and Means. Around the turn of the last century, Sand Mountain became enveloped in a supernatural aura. As with Brown Mountain in North Carolina, reports of strange lights began circulating along the roadways, just as automobiles were starting to replace horse-drawn vehicles as the primary means of transportation. The Brown Mountain lights were explained away in 1922 by United States Geological Survey (USGS) scientists, who posited that eyewitnesses were actually seeing the distant headlights of trains and cars. Following the publication of this theory, a number of fanciful backstories have sprung up throughout the remainder of the twentieth century as alternatives to the scientific explanation. In one of the stories, the lights are the unquiet spirits of a woman and her baby who were murdered on the mountain.

Interestingly enough, the Sand Mountain lights have not generated a large body of legends. The testimonies of people who encountered the lights suggested that they seemed to be entities that intentionally followed them up or down the mountain. Sightings of the lights diminished as more and more people moved to Sand Mountain. Many people have written off the lights as nothing more than glowing balls of methane gas. Nevertheless, reports of strange goings-on at Sand Mountain continue. Many of them are posted on websites like The Black Triangle, where people have reported hearing strange sounds and seeing a white creature that lopes along the old logging roads. One eyewitness described the lights as "a camera flash in the woods." He added that the graveyard near his house is a particularly mysterious place. However, the majority of the sightings posted on the Internet these days are made by writers who long to have the same ghostly experience on the mountain that their parents or grandparents had.

HOT ROD HAVEN (LOUISVILLE)

Hot Rod Haven is one of those urban legends that grew out of America's love affair with the automobile. In the standard variant of the legend, a young couple was driving to a dance. They met their fate on a winding stretch of road that has come to be known as Hot Rod Haven. As the young man drove his car around the curves and sped down the straightaway, he crashed at the bottom of the hill, where the road makes an abrupt left turn. Fittingly, the couple was interred in a private burial ground for the Mitchell and Griffen families at the top of the hill. In most of the versions of the tale, the girl's name is either Mary or Sarah. The young man's name is unknown. People say that the spirit of the young woman wanders through the cemetery at night, waiting for her boyfriend to take her to the dance.

In 2000, an investigator with the Louisville Ghost Hunters Society, Keith Age, explored the truth behind the legend by poring through the records of Jefferson County. He discovered that an accident similar to the one in the legend actually did occur on Hot Rod Haven. On September 23, 1946, Sarah Mitchell and her date, Roy Clarke, were on their way to a dance. Roy was driving too fast and lost control of his car, crashing as he tried to make the turn at the bottom of the hill. Keith then went to the cemetery at the top of the hill and found a stone marker engraved with the names of the young couple and the date: September 23, 1946.

In an article written by Chad Mills for WDRB.com, St. Anthony's Road (aka "Hot Rod Haven") acquired its reputation between the 1940s and the 1970s, when teenagers used it as a drag strip. The hazards of driving along this curvy road near Waverly Hills in southwest Louisville were aggravated when a landslide washed away a section of it. In the spring of 2020, plans were underway to install a concrete wedge on St. Anthony's Church Road. It is unlikely, though, that making the infamous road safer will diminish the appeal of the legend of Hot Rod Haven.

THE GHOSTS OF MAMMOTH CAVE
(EDMONSON, HART AND BARREN COUNTIES)

Not surprisingly, the history of tourism and the stories of haunted activity inside Mammoth Cave go hand in hand. Tourism in the cave began when Dr. John Croghan bought it in 1839 for $10,000. One of the slaves who was part of the purchase was Stephen Bishop, who became a tour guide, owing to his extensive knowledge of the cave. In the years Bishop spent exploring the cave on his own, he acquired a staggering amount of knowledge regarding its geological formations, as well as the fish, animals and insects that called it home. In fact, Bishop is credited with discovering over twenty miles of passages. Dr. Croghan granted Bishop his freedom in 1855. Sadly, the ex-slave died in 1856. Bishop and some of the other slaves who served as tour guides were buried, appropriately, in the Old Guide Cemetery. Some of the present employees of Mammoth Cave believe that Stephen Bishop and his colleagues were so dedicated that their disembodied footsteps occasionally echo through the labyrinth of passageways. The ghost of one of these guides appeared holding a

A slave named Stephen Bishop led the first tours through Mammoth Cave. *Courtesy of Wikimedia Commons.*

This vertical shaft is one of the many wonders of Mammoth Cave. *Courtesy of Wikimedia Commons.*

lantern on top of a rock formation called Sacrifice Rock. Tourists and guides recalled that the figure was wearing a long-sleeved shirt and a wide-brimmed hat.

Some of the other ghostly sounds may have their source in the period when Dr. Croghan established a tuberculosis hospital inside the cave. He was convinced that the cave's fifty-four-degree temperatures could aid in curing consumption. The fifteen patients who came to the cave for treatment lived in eleven huts. Patients who succumbed to the disease were laid out on a slab of rock known as "Corpse Rock." The coughing sounds that some visitors and employees have heard in this part of the cave are believed to be the last gasps of Dr. Croghan's patients, none of whom were cured.

According to the website National Parks Traveler, a number of the ghosts manifest themselves during the blackouts. At this point in the tours, the lights are turned off and a ranger guides the tourists through the cave using only a lantern. A number of rangers claim to have been touched, grabbed or pushed when the lights are off and no one else is around. During one of the tours, guide Larry Pursell noticed a Black family at the back of the tour group. He recalled that the father was wearing a white Panama hat. They appeared to be listening intently to the guide. Toward the end of the tour, Pursell turned off the lights and continued his narration. When he turned the lights back on, the family was gone.

Undoubtedly, the cave's most famous ghost is the spirit of Floyd Collins. On January 30, 1925, the spelunker was attempting to find an entrance to Mammoth Cave by himself. He was trying to squeeze through a small hole when he knocked over his lamp. At the same time, he accidentally knocked a rock loose. The rock fell on his leg, trapping him in the cave. Before long, word of his predicament spread through the community, and rescuers rushed to the cave. They were able to keep him alive by dropping food and water through a rescue shaft they had dug. Around the same time, vendors and newspaper reporters converged on the site, eager to score an interview with the intrepid explorer. One of them, William Burke Miller, managed to make his way through Collins's hole several times to talk to him. Miller's interview eventually won him a Pulitzer Prize. On February 4, the unthinkable happened: the roof of the cave collapsed. A second rescue shaft was dug, but by the time the rescuers were able to extricate Collins, he had died. His body was removed with a great deal of effort, and his funeral was held inside the cave. Collins was buried just outside of the cave. Incredibly, the new owners exhumed Collins's body two years later and exhibited his corpse in a glass coffin in nearby Crystal Cave. Collins's family finally regained possession of his body and reburied him.

According to the website Atlas Obscura, Floyd Collins is still very much attached to the cave where he spent his last moments. Tour guide Colleen Olson recalled a caver who had entered a part of the cave where Collins had spent a great deal of time exploring. Suddenly, the caver tripped on a rock. She was about to plummet to the dark recesses below when someone grabbed her arm and pulled her back up. Thinking that her partner had come to her aid, she looked around and saw him on the other side of the cave. At that moment, she realized that she had been saved from certain death by the ghost of Floyd Collins.

STELLA'S GHOST IN THE C.C. COHEN BUILDING (PADUCAH)

The structure known as the C.C. Cohen building was erected in 1865 for M. Livingston & Company. Several different businesses operated from this building throughout the twentieth century. In the early 1900s, a dry-goods store was located here. In 1914, P.L. Peacher Liquor Dealers and the Renkopf Distilling Company moved in. In 1921, the C.C. Cohen family purchased the building. Following the murder of her husband in an alley in 1961, Stella Cohen Peine and her sister Goldie Cohen lived in their second-floor apartment. After Goldie's death in 1974, Stella lived alone until she died in the apartment in 1980. Alan Raidt owned the building for several years in the early 2000s until his death. It houses a popular eatery, Shandies restaurant, and—some people say—Stella's restless spirit.

Stella's ghost has made its presence known in a variety of ways. It is not unusual at all for employees to open Shandies in the morning and find that all of the chairs have been moved around and the salt and pepper shakers have been emptied out on the tables. Sometimes, signs and lights are unplugged for no apparent reason. Waitstaff and customers have reported seeing drinks move across the bar on their own. One morning, the owner found an onion on each table.

Stella's full-body apparition has been sighted as well. Most of the time, she has been seen staring out of the window of her second-floor apartment. In an article published in the *Paducah Sun* in 2019, co-owner Karla Lawrence reported the sighting of an entirely different type of spirit by a couple from

Left: The C.C. Cohen Building was constructed for M. Livingston & Company in 1865. *Courtesy of Marilyn Brown.*

Right: The ghost of Stella Cohen Peine haunts Shandies restaurant in the C.C. Cohen Building. *Courtesy of Marilyn Brown.*

out of town: "It was real icy and wintery out and the couple was standing up here at the bar. They were just eating when the wife jumped up all of the sudden and said, 'A white Doberman just brushed past my leg.'" Interestingly enough, Stella owned two white Doberman Pinschers. No other dogs were in the restaurant at the time.

A former employee named Robyn Shapiro had a particularly startling encounter with Stella's ghost late one evening. After counting the money in her drawer, Robyn placed a pair of scissors on top of the clock: "I went back to the office, picked something up and walked back to the register, and the pair of scissors flew across the room and hit the floor, close behind me." Robyn also claims to have smelled Stella's perfume as she passed by on the third floor. Robyn even suspects that Stella tried to trip her on one occasion.

Not everyone who works at Shandies has had good reason to be afraid. Co-owner David Jones does not believe that Stella is a malicious entity: "I think she just likes hanging around and checking things out." In fact, some of the customers seem to enjoy eating in the presence of Stella's vigilant ghost.

THE LOUISVILLE FREE PUBLIC LIBRARY (LOUISVILLE)

The Louisville Free Public Library is the largest public library system in the state of Kentucky. The Main Library at Fourth and York Streets is listed in the National Register of Historic Places. According to the nomination form, the Main Library was funded by Andrew Carnegie in 1906. Designed in the Beaux-Arts style by the New York architecture firm Tachau and Pilcher, the two-and-a-half story building was constructed from Bowling Green limestone in a T-shaped plan. The two-story portico dominates the main façade. Two identical wings flank the entrance. Below the windows on the first floor is the name of a discipline; lions' heads protrude from the sills of windows on the second floor. The base of the *T* is formed by the rear of the library. In 1908, a museum was opened in the basement of the Main Library. It was relocated to the Montessori School for a short time because of the damage caused by the flood of 1937. The Main Library suffered severe water damage a second time in August 2009, the result of a heavy deluge that poured seven inches of rain on the city in only seventy-five minutes. The storm inflicted approximately $5 million worth of damage to the old building. Because the Louisville Free Public Library has survived the worst that nature seems capable of, it is likely to be around for a long time.

Like many libraries in the South and in other parts of the country, the Louisville Free Public Library is said to be haunted by the dutiful ghost of a deceased librarian. In the book *Phantoms of Old Louisville*, Sam Loftus, a former employee, told author David Domine about an apparition he encountered while walking through the stacks at 9:00 p.m. one summer night just before the library was locked up. Loftus was making his rounds to make sure no one was still in the building. "It was like she was just going about her business of putting the books back in place," Loftus said. "She had on round spectacles and her hair was up in a bun, and she wore a high-waisted, long skirt and a long-sleeved blouse." The specter, clearly from another time, stared at Loftus for a few seconds with a puzzled look on its face before fading away. Understandably, Loftus decided to cut short his walk-through of the library and immediately walked out the door.

So many librarians have worked at the Louisville Free Public Library over the last century that is it is difficult to select one particular woman whose spirit is still "on the job," even after death. However, a likely candidate is the library's first head of reference, Marilla Waite Freeman, who held that position for five years. In that short time, she became one of the most

A former employee saw the ghost of a librarian at the Louisville Free Public Library.

prominent librarians in the state. Is it possible that Ms. Freeman is so integral a part of the history of the old library that she is still making sure that everything is running as smoothly as it was when she worked there?

THE DUPONT MANSION (LOUISVILLE)

The DuPont family became one of the wealthiest families in Delaware by manufacturing gunpowder in the War of 1812 and the Civil War. In 1854, two members of the family, Biederman and Alfred Victor DuPont, decided to explore the business opportunities in Louisville, Kentucky. Within a few months, they had established AV DuPont and Company, which specialized in the production of paper and gunpowder. In 1870, Biederman bought the home of Reverend Stuart Robinson at the top of a hill. He opened his front yard to the public as a park, which eventually became Central Park. His brother Alfred Victor spent most of his time at his suite in the Galt House Hotel, where he could entertain his lady friends away from the

The ghost of Alfred Victor DuPont is reputed to continue his womanizing ways at the DuPont bed-and-breakfast.

prying eyes of neighbors. In 1879, the brothers built a three-story Italianate mansion at 1317 South Fourth Street as a "home away from home" for visiting relatives and business associates. Alfred Victor stayed at the DuPont Mansion only for scheduled visits with Biederman. When the number of visitors to the South Fourth Street mansion began to decline, the family sold it to Thomas Prather Jacob in 1886. In 1893, Alfred Victor's secret life came crashing down around him when Maggie Payne, the madam of a local bordello, informed him on the porch of the Galt Hotel that she was pregnant with his child. Concerned with the damage this revelation could do to his family's reputation, he vehemently denied her accusation and ordered her to leave. Maggie pulled a pistol and shot Alfred Victor, killing him instantly. The DuPont family tried to cover up the sordid truth behind Alfred Victor's death by informing the police that he died of a heart attack at the Galt Hotel. The facts in the case did not come to light until the 1930s. By the 1990s, the mansion had become a dilapidated shadow of its former splendor. At this time, efforts were undertaken to stabilize it. In the 2000s, the Warrens restored the DuPont Mansion and converted it into a popular bed-and-breakfast, where people can experience the luxury of sleeping and dining in a Victoria-era palatial townhouse.

According to David Domine, author of *Phantoms of Old Louisville*, Alfred Victor's tenuous connection to the Dupont Mansion has extended far after his death. In the 1990s, a local subcontractor named Ronald Haycraft was working in the old house by himself. He was standing at the bottom of the staircase when, all at once, he felt like someone was watching him. He looked around and then resumed work on his project. A few minutes later, he looked up and beheld a spectral figure that shook him to his core. He said that the apparition, which resembled an average-looking man in an old-fashioned tuxedo, "shimmered and shook as if someone had dropped a pebble in the water and caused ripples that distorted the reflection." Before the specter faced away, Haycraft noticed a dark red stain on its chest.

Domine reports that an interior decorator named Geraldine Beck also had an unnerving encounter with Alfred Victor's ghost around the same time. She was walking down the staircase, and as she neared the bottom, she felt someone blow in her ear. The next day, Beck was walking down the same staircase when she saw a man wearing an old-fashioned tuxedo and a top hat walk in front of her. As soon as he vanished, she screamed and ran into the other room. On her third day in the house, Beck was walking down the staircase once again. She breathed a sigh of relief when she reached the bottom and nothing happened. At that same moment, she felt a hand grab her by the buttocks. She took off running and never used the stairs again during her time at the mansion. Beck became a firm believer in the stories she had heard about Alfred Victor's womanizing ways.

THE PALACE THEATRE (LOUISVILLE)

Built by the Austrian American architect John Eberson, the 3,300-seat Louisville Palace Theatre opened its doors on September 1, 1928. The lobby of the Baroque movie theater was embellished by 140 carvings of famous historical figures, including Eberson himself. The theater's grand one-thousand-pipe Wurlitzer organ was a fixture until 1978. The Louisville Palace Theatre fell victim to the declining popularity of old movie houses amid the rise of suburban multiplexes in the 1970s and closed its doors. John Siegel reopened the theater as a live entertainment venue in 1981, but it closed in 1985 because of the high cost of maintaining and restoring it. Sunshine Theater Inc. reopened it in 1994. Live Nation reopened the theater in 2005. Today, audiences flock to live performances at the Louisville Palace Theatre, which is the only grand movie house still standing in Louisville.

Like many of the historical movie houses, the Louisville Palace Theatre has a haunted history. One of the specters that frequents the theater wears a gray dress and shoulder pads as she walks up the staircase. She usually fades away just before she reaches the top. The most frequently sighted female spirit is the Lady in Gray. In fact, most of the staff at the theater have encountered her in one way or another. With her hair in a tight bun, she wears a white gown with white gloves. She appears to be holding a book or playbill. The Lady in Gray is most commonly seen walking down the first aisle. One of the theater's male ghosts is the spirit of a projectionist who had a heart attack and fell down the stairs as he was being carried away. "Bernie," as he is affectionately called, is often seen walking through the spotlight on the stage. He has also been known to tap the female employees on the shoulder and shove male employees. Another male specter is the spirit of an older man who was sighted during the restoration in the 1990s sitting in the balcony. He was wearing work clothes and glasses and had his hair in a flattop. He has also been heard whistling in the theater. A crew member who had fallen asleep on the scaffolding while painting the ceiling claimed to have been awakened by the voice of an older man, who told him to "wake up." The most rarely sighted apparitions in the theater are the ghosts of two mischievous children. Their footsteps have been heard running through the theater at night. Apparently, not everyone connected with the old theater has permanently exited the building.

The ghosts of children and a worker named Bernie haunt the Palace Theatre.

WAVERLY HILLS SANATORIUM (LOUISVILLE)

Waverly Hills Sanatorium is located on the site of a one-room schoolhouse established by Major Thomas H. Hays in 1883. The teacher, Lizzie Lee Harris, named the school after Sir Walter Scott's Waverly novels. Built in 1908 on Waverly Hill, Waverly Tuberculosis Sanatorium started out as a two-story frame building. When it opened on July 26, 1910, it could accommodate 40 to 50 patients. As tuberculosis spread through Jefferson County, the number of patients at the sanatorium ballooned to 140. Construction on a much larger building commenced in 1924 and was completed on October 17, 1926. Waverly Hills Sanatorium operated as a self-sufficient institution with its own water-treatment facility and post office. Staff and patients planted and harvested vegetables. Even cattle were brought to supply the patients' need for meat. The number of patients declined drastically in 1961 following the discovery of streptomycin, which was used to treat and cure tuberculosis. The next year, a geriatric clinic called Woodhaven Medical Services moved into the building. The state closed Woodhaven in 1981. For the next twenty

Approximately 8,212 patients died of tuberculosis at Waverly Hills Sanatorium in a fifty-year period.

Behind these "vacant, eye-like windows," restless phantoms walk the halls of Waverly Hills Tuberculosis Sanatorium.

years, the abandoned building was heavily vandalized. In 2001, Charles and Tina Mattingly purchased the Waverly Hills Sanitarium with the intention of restoring it. They have been assisted in their efforts by the Waverly Hills Historical Society, which has opened it to the general public for tours and paranormal investigations.

The vandalism that has taken such a heavy toll on the building has actually enhanced the "creep factor." Staff members and ghost hunters have encountered the spirits of an angry old man and a little boy named Timmy who plays with balls that are put in the building for his amusement. Visitors have seen the spirit of a little girl running through the third-floor solarium. The sounds of slamming doors and disembodied footsteps echo throughout the building. Ghost-hunting groups have photographed a large number of orbs in the body chute, through which the bodies of deceased patients were transported at night out of view of the rest of the patients. Doors have a tendency to open up on their own. The kitchen is one of the most haunted places in the old hospital. Not only has the ghost of a man in a white coat been sighted in the kitchen, but the unmistakable aroma of baked bread wafts through the hallway occasionally. The most legendary room is 502, where a twenty-nine-year-old nurse is believed to have hanged herself from a light fixture. According to another legend, a nurse jumped to her death from the roof patio in 1932.

The high levels of paranormal activity reported at Waverly Hills are probably due to the fact that approximately 8,212 patients died there. The pain and suffering the patients endured at Waverly Hills Sanatorium may have left an indelible imprint on its walls and hallways. Not surprisingly, the historic hospital has been featured on a number of television shows, including *Ghost Adventures*, *Scariest Places on Earth* and *Ghost Hunters*.

Chapter 6

LEGENDARY LOST TREASURE

THE LEGEND OF THE SPRINKLE DOLLARS (LEWIS COUNTY)

Lost mines have been the stuff of legend. One of the South's most tantalizing treasure stories can be found in the wilds of Lewis County. The story goes that in 1775, Indians attacked a group of men who were exploring the region, leaving only a man named McCormick alive. They took him prisoner and returned him to their camp, where they tied him to a tree. Just before McCormick was burned alive, a group of French missionaries who lived with the Indians talked them into setting him free. His story attracted the attention of a number of small communities in the area. Eventually, a band of French settlers who were led to the Indian tribe by the missionaries learned of the location of a large vein of silver from the Indians. The men found the vein and mined it for the next two to three years. They also set up a smelter to melt the silver into bars. Within a few months, they were joined by several other settlers, one of whom was Josiah Sprinkle. Mining operations ceased during the Revolutionary War, when the Indians went on the attack. The exact location of the mine was lost.

Years later, in the 1830s, Josiah Sprinkle showed up in Mason County, Kentucky, with a buckskin bag of silver dollars. The store owners who accepted the coins from the old man noticed immediately that they were not produced by any of the U.S. mints. The silver dollars had an owl on one side and a six-pointed star on the other. They were larger and thicker than standard U.S. coins. He told the merchants that he made the dollars himself and that he mined the silver from his own mine. However, Sprinkle refused to tell anyone the location of the mine.

Within the space of a few weeks, Sprinkle was arrested by government agents and taken to court. A close inspection of the coins revealed that they were pure silver, without alloy. At the end of the trial, Sprinkle was acquitted. Legend has it that he paid his attorney with a bag of Sprinkle dollars. He continued to mine the silver and make his own silver dollars until the day he died. To this day, no one knows where his mine was located.

THE LOST TREASURE OF THE CUMBERLAND GAP (MIDDLESBORO)

During the Civil War, both Union and Confederate forces fought for control of the Cumberland Gap. The Union army believed that capturing the Cumberland Gap would cut the Confederacy in half and disrupt supply lines. Most of the fighting took the form of skirmishes instead of large-scale battles. Union forces under the command of Major General Ambrose Burnside eventually wrested the gap from the Confederacy on September 9, 1863.

The best-known legend to emerge from this conflict began when an epidemic of measles resulted in the quarantine of a complete regiment of Confederate soldiers for several weeks. The story goes that four of these men decided to rob the Confederate payroll and pin the blame on the Yankees. After nightfall, the four soldiers attacked the pay wagon, killing the paymaster and guards. They then took the money and drove the wagon and horses into a ravine. Before returning to camp, the men hid the payroll. They planned to return to the hiding place and retrieve the money at a later time.

A few months after the end of the Civil War, an ex-Confederate soldier who identified himself only as Jones returned to the site of the Confederate camp in the Cumberland Gap and began searching for the hidden payroll. After looking for a month, he found the hidden money. Fearing that the federal government or soldiers in his former regiment would shoot him and take the money, Jones left it where he had found it.

He returned to the hotel in Middlesboro where he had been staying and told his story. He said that three of the four soldiers who had stolen the payroll were killed in action in Virginia. The fourth was severely wounded.

As he lay dying, he told Jones that the payroll was placed in a trunk and hidden in a cave. A few days later, Jones left the hotel and never returned to Middlesboro. No one knows where the money is.

The Lost Treasure of Pilot Rock
(Christian County)

In 1888, two wealthy farmers, Samuel Henderson and Joshua Tucker, were living in the northeast section of Christian County. South of their farms was a large sandstone rock, approximately two hundred feet in diameter, known as Pilot Rock. At this time, two brothers, Coy and Clyde Fields, worked as farmhands for Henderson and Tucker. In the fall of 1889, Coy overheard Tucker tell his wife that he was going to hide the $3,000 he had received from the sale of his tobacco in one of the flour barrels in the pantry. Coy rushed back to his brother and hatched a plan to steal the gold. Clyde then talked Henderson's young wife, Flora, into helping him steal her husband's profits from the sale of his tobacco crop, which amounted to $2,000. After the theft, the three planned to flee to Chicago.

A few days later, Clyde told Flora to steal her husband's money and have a saddled horse in the barn ready for them to ride off on. She kept her part of the bargain, bringing Henderson's money to the barn, but Clyde tied her up and gagged her and left her in the barn. He rode away on the horse to Pilot Rock, where he and his brother had planned to meet up. After a few minutes, Flora got loose and told her husband that Clyde had stolen the money. The irate husband mounted his horse and rode off in pursuit of Clyde.

Coy's attempted robbery was less successful. He emptied two barrels of flour on the floor before finding the one with the money. He had just picked up the bag of coins when Tucker burst into the kitchen with a lantern. In his hurry to escape, Coy slipped on the flour and fell to the floor. As Tucker was aiming his gun, Coy ran through the back door. At the same time, Tucker fired his gun, barely missing Coy. The thief had escaped, but Tucker had no trouble tracking him, because he left a trail of flour behind as he ran all the way to Pilot Rock.

Coy and Clyde spent the night on top of Pilot Rock. At dawn, the brothers started climbing down the crevice in the rock. Armed with a shotgun and a rifle, Henderson and Tucker fired at the farmhands, killing both of them.

Locals believe that Coy and Clyde Fields hid $2,000 somewhere around Pilot Rock. *Courtesy of Wikimedia Commons.*

They combed Pilot Rock, the crevice and the area around Pilot Rock but found nothing more than a few coins that the thieves had probably dropped in their hurry to escape. The rest of the gold is probably still buried in the woods around Pilot Rock.

DOCK BROWN'S OUTLAW GOLD (GRAYSON COUNTY)

The legend of Grayson County's outlaw gold begins with John Hooper, who fled to Kentucky in 1840 after killing a man in Tennessee. While his wife and children remained in Tennessee, Hooper changed his name to John Brown and purchased over one hundred acres of land near Pine Knob, north of Causeyville. In 1842, two of his sons, Pickney and Culliam, left Tennessee and joined up with their father in Kentucky.

Like their father, Pickney and Culliam decided to live outside of the law. They changed their names to P.H. and Dock Brown, respectively, and, along with their father, murdered and robbed anyone who came their way. It was said that anyone who spent the night at their house never returned home.

All three men were scoundrels, but Dock was the worst of the bunch. His first robbery was the theft of $150 in gold and $900 in bank notes from a man named Frank Pugh. Through cattle rustling, murder and robbery, he amassed around $50,000. Dock was believed to have hidden much of his money in Big Mouth Cave on the north side of Pine Knob. Interestingly enough, not only has none of the treasure ever been found, but also few people have actually looked for it.

JONATHAN SWIFT'S LOST SILVER MINE (EASTERN KENTUCKY)

Most people think of Jonathan Swift as the author of *Gulliver's Travels*. However, a much more legendary figure by the same name can be found in the folklore of eastern Kentucky. The primary source of the legend of Swift's silver mine is a journal that he is said to have written and left to the widow of Joseph Renfro of Bean's Station, Tennessee. Following Renfro's murder at the hands of marauding Indians, Swift is believed to have embarked on a love affair with Renfro's wife. Swift claimed to have come to Kentucky from England in 1760, well ahead of Daniel Boone. One day, he wounded a bear and followed it into a cave. As he looked around in the light of his torch, he was amazed at the sight of a vein of silver in the cave walls. For the next five years, Swift made periodic trips to the cave, where he mined the silver. According to James Lane Allen, the author of an article published in *Harper's Magazine* in 1886, Swift "made silver in large quantities, burying some thirty thousand dollars and crowns on a large creek; fifteen thousand dollars a little way off, near some trees, which were duly marked; a prize of six thousand dollars close by the fork of a white oak; and three thousand dollars in the rocks of a rock house: all which, in these notes, it is allowed anyone who will [hunt for it]."

In his journal, Smith wrote that he had to stop mining the silver after a series of attacks by local Indian tribes. He sealed up the cave and left the area. He intended to return and resume his mining operation after the Indian "trouble" had died down, but he lost his sight in his later years and was unable to pinpoint the exact location of the cave.

For many years, treasure hunters have searched every county in eastern Tennessee for Smith's silver mine. The fact that no silver was ever found has led some to believe that Swift's lost silver mine is nothing more than a legend created by the poor mountain people of eastern Kentucky whose misery was alleviated, at least partially, by the possibility that riches were buried in one of the many caves in the area. In addition, there is no proof that Swift's journal really exists.

However, not everyone subscribes to the belief that Swift's mine is nothing more than a story. Writing for LEX-18 television in Lexington, author Michael Berk wrote about a treasure hunter named William Sharp, who is convinced that there actually is a mine on a cliff somewhere in Lincoln County. His search began with the discovery of steel wheels that belonged to carts used to transport silver ore from Swift's mine. He later found the word *mine* carved into a stone and an antique drill bit that may have been part of a hand crank. These findings, which were made in the course of a year, have fueled Sharp's desire to prove that Swift's mine is much more than a mountain myth.

Chapter 7

MYSTERIES FROM THE SKIES

THE GREAT KENTUCKY MEAT STORM
(OLYMPIAN SPRINGS)

Mysterious "falls" from the sky are nothing new. In 1794, hundreds of toads fell out of the sky, striking 150 French soldiers near Lalain, France. In September 1857, strange sugar crystals fell from the sky in Lake County, California. On June 16, 1940, people living in Meschera, Russia, were simultaneously puzzled and delighted by a fall of sixteenth-century coins, probably part of a cache that had been uncovered and scooped up by winds. Undoubtedly, the Great Kentucky Meat Storm is one of the most bizarre of this type of airborne phenomenon.

On March 3, 1876, Mrs. Crouch was making soap outside of her house when she saw pieces of some sort of meat falling from the sky like large snowflakes. The only other witness to this eerie event was her grandson. Within a matter of minutes, the five-thousand-square-foot yard was blanketed with slivers of flesh ranging in size from two to four inches. Later, she told a reporter from the *New York Herald* that "the storm, by measure, would not go into a half bushel." She also told the reporter that the flakes of meat, which fell at a straight or sloping angle, were eaten by the family dog, which became sick afterward. Two of the locals who stopped by and sampled the meat told Mrs. Crouch that it tasted like venison or mutton.

After the story appeared in the *New York Times* on March 9, a number of experts offered their opinions as to the identity of the meat. Leopold

Brandeis analyzed a sample of the substance, preserved in glycerine, and determined that it was nostoc, a type of cyanobacteria that swells up to a jelly-like glob after a rain. He turned the sample over to Dr. Allan McLane of the Newark Scientific Association. He concurred with histologist Dr. A. Mead Edwards that the meat was lung tissue from a horse or human baby. However, L.D. Kastenbine, MD, a professor of chemistry at the Louisville College of Pharmacy, hypothesized that the meat had been consumed and vomited out by a flock of vultures flying over the far. This theory was first offered by a hunter named B.F. Ellington, who declared that the meat was bear meat that had probably been disgorged by vultures, which are known to regurgitate half-digested meat in the presence of predators, either while flying or just before taking off. To many biologists today, this is the most logical explanation.

THE EXTRATERRESTRIAL TRAIN WRECK (PAINTSVILLE)

On January 14, 2002, at 2:47 a.m., a CSX train loaded with sixteen thousand tons of coal was headed toward Shelbiana from Russell. As the train neared a solid rock bluff at Milepost 42, the conductor saw a cluster of lights around the bend. A few moments later, the lights seemed to be spotlights scanning the river. All at once, the train's onboard computer began to turn off at lightning speed, causing the electrical systems to fail. Another train had the same electrical malfunction. At the same time, the first train braked; however, because of the trains' heavy loads, it took two miles for both of them to come to a complete stop. When the alarm bells rang, the engineer noticed three flying objects with searchlights, one of which was hovering about ten to twelve feet above the track. As the train coasted around the corner, it struck one of the objects. The engineer said that it was eighteen to twenty feet long and silver in color. The object peeled several pieces off the train.

The crew drove the damaged train to the rail yard. The engines and two cars were removed from each train. The story goes that before the members of the crew could be interviewed by railroad officials, they were intercepted by a "man in black," who interviewed them and left the yard immediately after. The crews were then taken to Martin, Kentucky, where they were interviewed, drug tested and instructed not to speak to reporters. The media was informed that the train was damaged in a rockslide. Eventually, of course, the story of a UFO encounter leaked, thanks to the Internet and social media. To this day, many people believe that the coal train actually did run into a UFO on January 14, 2002.

WAS CAPTAIN THOMAS MANTELL SHOT DOWN BY A UFO? (FORT KNOX)

By the late 1940s, sightings of unidentified flying objects were being reported with some regularity. A number of government officials credited these sightings to "war nerves," especially those of UFOs observed by pilots. However, the general public and the authorities began taking UFOs more seriously following the Mantell UFO incident.

In 1948, Thomas Mantell was a twenty-five-year-old captain in the Kentucky National Guard. A former air force pilot, Mantell logged 2,167 hours of flying time in World War II, serving in the Battle of Normandy. He had had many encounters with hostile aircraft, but they were nothing like the object he encountered on January 7, 1948. Sergeant Quinton Black of the Kentucky Highway Patrol informed Goodman Airfield of his sighting of a flying object near Madisonville, Kentucky, at 1:45 p.m. Two eyewitnesses in the control tower at the base described it as white in color. Base commander Guy Hix said that the object was stationary for one and a half hours. Captain Mantell's P-51 Mustang and three F-51D Mustangs were ordered to fly toward the object. After one of the planes ran low on fuel and returned to the base, the other three planes continued chasing the object. After a few minutes, two of the other pilots called off the pursuit, but Mantell's plane continued to climb into the clouds. According to the official U.S. Air Force report, Mantell blacked out from lack of oxygen at twenty-five thousand feet and crashed on a farm near Franklin, Kentucky. The watch that the firemen retrieved from Mantell's corpse was stopped at 3:18 p.m., the time of the crash.

The incident was reported in newspapers across the country. A number of alternative explanations for the crash were bantered around locally and in the media. Among these theories was the claim that the flying object was actually a Soviet missile. The most persistent rumor was that Mantell's Mustang was shot down by a flying saucer. Owing to a lack of evidence, the air force rejected all of these explanations, including the stories about the wreckage's high radioactive levels.

Flying a P-51 Mustang like the one pictured here, Captain Thomas Mantell is said to have been shot down by a UFO in 1948. *Courtesy of Wikimedia Commons.*

In 1948, the U.S. Air Force appointed a special task force called Project Sign to investigate the Mantell incident. Noted astrologer Dr. J. Allen Hynek, an advisor to Project Sign, suggested that Mantell was pursuing the planet Venus by mistake. However, in 1952, Dr. Hynek rejected the Venus explanation, because the planet was not visible at the time. Even if conditions were favorable, Venus would have appeared as only a pinpoint of light. That same year, the air force's Project Blue Book proposed the theory that Mantell might have actually been chasing a Skyhook balloon, which measured radiation levels in the atmosphere. Mantell's plane crash fired the public's imagination and fueled the widely held belief that UFOs were not only real but also meant to do us harm.

THE VALLEY HILL LIGHTS (VALLEY HILL)

Sightings of the Virgin Mary date back centuries. Most of these appearances have occurred in Europe, especially Italy, France, southern Germany and Belgium. The most famous of the European Marian sightings are Our Lady of Fatima and Our Lady of Lourdes. Other examples include Our Lady of Guadalupe and Our Lady of Knock. The United States leads the rest of the world in the total number of Marian appearances. One of them took place in Valley Hill, Kentucky.

On October 27, 1995, the television show *Unsolved Mysteries* broadcast an episode about strange appearances in the sky over Valley Hill, Kentucky. Most of the phenomena consisted of explosions of colorful patterns of light and what appeared to be dots. Some eyewitnesses claim to have seen "golden flakes" on the faces of the other "stargazers." Iona Wright was the first person in the area to claim to have seen visions at Valley Hill. Over the years, several other people have said that visions appeared to them in the area.

On April 6, 1995, a Sunday school teacher named Ann Mudd and eight of her students were treated to a spectacular sight at Valley Hill. Several of the students noticed weird colors circling the sun, which appeared to be pulsating. A few moments later, the faces of the girls seemed to be covered in traces of gold. The Polaroid photographs Mudd took of the girls showed much more than strange colors. In one of the photographs, the images of Jesus and Mary with a veil were present. In a second picture, one of the girls seemed to be surrounded by angels. Another girl recognized the name of her cousin on a tombstone in one of the photographs. Skeptics in Valley Hill became believers after they began having visions.

Dr. Joe Nickell, a writer for *Skeptical Inquirer*, debunked the photographs with logical explanations. He said that the writing on the tombstone was actually on a chart on the back of the photo pack. Nickell wrote off the appearances of Jesus and Mary as nothing more than pareidolia, which is the tendency of the human mind to impose logical interpretations on random visual stimulation. Finally, he claimed that a leaky cartridge created the "angels" flying around one of the girls. Reports of bizarre colors in the sky have died down over time, but the mystery of the 1995 sightings endures, despite the article in the *Skeptical Inquirer*.

THE STANFORD ALIEN ABDUCTION (STANFORD)

On January 6, Mona Stafford decided to go with two of her friends, Elaine Thomas and Louise Smith, to the Redwoods Restaurant between Stanford and Lancaster to celebrate her birthday. Louise Smith drove her friends to the restaurant in her 1967 Chevy Nova. After dinner, the three women left the restaurant at 11:15 p.m. When they reached Stanford, they turned onto Highway 79 from Highway 78. They were just a few miles outside of Stanford when Mona spotted a bright red object in the sky. She immediately dismissed her initial notion that the object was a burning airplane when the strange craft landed ahead of their car on the right side of the road about one hundred yards away. The women recalled that the object was bigger than two houses. After rocking for a few seconds, the object moved to the left.

Terrified, the women drove off. When they had driven a quarter of a mile, they realized from the blue light shining in the rear window that the object was now behind them. All at once, some invisible force wrested control of the car from Louise. Within just a few moments, the car had reached a speed of eighty-five miles per hour. Mona, who was sitting in the front passenger seat, was unable to help Louise take control of the car. Simultaneously, both women experienced an intense burning in their eyes. Their blood pressure rose when they realized that the car was moving at a high rate of speed, even though the ignition lights indicated that the vehicle had stalled. In a matter of seconds, the women were on Highway 78 near Hustonville, eight miles from where they had just been. They were shocked when their watches showed that an hour and twenty minutes had elapsed from the time when their encounter had begun.

It was an hour and a half later when Louise's car reached her trailer. Once the women were inside, they realized that their necks were inflamed and their eyes seemed to be on fire. The pain intensified when Louise washed her face with water. Jim, an artist, made three sketches based on each of the women's descriptions of the object. The sketches appeared to be similar. The women then contacted the police department and the navy office, but none of the authorities took their stories very seriously.

In the days that followed, the women's medical problems became much worse. Not only did the pain in Mona's eyes worsen, but she also contracted conjunctivitis. Louise's car developed serious problem with its electrical systems. In addition, her pet parakeet sensed that she had changed. It became frantic when she approached its cage; a few days later, it died.

After the navy office sent the story of the women's terrifying ordeal to the media, they were interviewed by Jerry Black of MUFON (the Mutual UFO Network). Around the same time, investigators from CUFOS (Center for UFO Studies) and APRO (Aerial Phenomena Research Organization) arrived at Stanford. They discovered that sightings of a UFO were reported in Casey and Lincoln Counties on the same night. A lie detector test administered by Lexington Police Department detective James Young indicated that all three women were telling the truth. On March 9, 1976, Dr. Leo Sprinkle of the University of Wyoming performed hypnotic regression on the women. They revealed that during the period of "lost time," they were taken aboard the strange craft and subjected to medical examinations by shadowy creatures. Investigators later determined that these strange creatures were actually aliens from another planet.

UFO "Shoot-out" over Louisville (Louisville)

The May 4, 1993 edition of the *Weekly World News* ran a cover story about a "two-minute dogfight" on a February night over Louisville. A policeman named Kenny Downs was in a police helicopter with pilot Kenny Graham, flying to the General Electric plant where a break-in was reported, when they encountered what seemed to be a ball of fire. On closer inspection, they could tell that the object was pear-shaped and about the size of a basketball. In the glare of the helicopter's spotlight, it appeared to have reached a height of about five hundred feet. After making two counterclockwise loops, it showed up behind the helicopter. Graham pushed the helicopter to a speed of one hundred miles an hour in an effort to elude the object. Nevertheless, it managed to pass the helicopter and soar above them. When Graham inched closer to the object, it emitted three basketball-sized fireballs that "fizzed out" before hitting the helicopter. After climbing hundreds of feet, the object disappeared in the distance.

The UFO incident soon became a media sensation. The *Louisville Courier-Journal* of March 4, 1993, ran the headline, "UFO Puts on Show: Jefferson County Police Officers Describe Close Encounter." The article described the UFO's movement as "drifting back and forth on a string." The writer added that the object circled the police helicopter several times. The story that was published in the May 4 edition of the *Weekly World News* referred to the helicopter-UFO incident as a "harrowing two-minute dogfight."

However, the *Courier*'s follow-up article, published on May 4, essentially debunked the March 4 article. According to the article, Scott Heacock and his wife, Conchys, created a hot-air balloon from a plastic dry-cleaning bag, balsa wood and a dozen birthday candles. They launched it the same night that the police helicopter reported its sighting. The writer of the article speculated that the force of the helicopter's props caused the balloon to move up and down. The fireballs propelled from the UFO were actually blobs of melted plastic or birthday candles that fell off the balloon. Because the candles were the "relighting" type, they would probably have been resistant to the prop wash. Heacock said that he witnessed the helicopter's encounter with his hot-air balloon. However, Kenny Downs disagreed with Heacock, stating, "I don't think six candles and a plastic bag can fly at the speed we flew." A large number of UFOlogists agree with him.

Mystery Lights on the Kentucky Border (Baskett)

On February 1, 2021, Evansville police officer Trendon D'mechi and his partner were sitting in their parked car at the intersection of Governor Street and Sweetser Avenue when they saw something highly unusual: a string of white lights that soared across the night sky. The lights appeared to be hovering over the state line in Baskett, Kentucky. D'mechi filmed the lights with his cellphone and posted the video to Facebook. The posting generated a lot of speculation but no real answers as to the identity of the lights. The next day, D'mechi posted, "My partner and I definitely felt uneasy after seeing the lights." D'mechi was also baffled by the fact that the department received no phone calls about strange lights in the sky the day of his sighting.

The director of marketing and air service for Evansville Regional Airport was perplexed, not only by the lights, but also by the police department's failure to notify her: "This is the first that I've heard or seen of it, and no, we aren't aware of anything in the area. Although, unless commercial, we aren't always made aware." A spokesman for Scott Air Force Base in western Illinois was unaware of any exercises involving aircraft that could have emitted the lights.

A number of theories have been proposed regarding the origin of the lights. One possibility is that drones emitted the lights. Satellites launched by Elon Musk's SpaceX Company were also proposed. While it is true that these satellites do resemble a pearl necklace, they do not fly as fast as the lights that appeared over Evansville on February 1.

THE BLUEGRASS UFO BLITZ OF 1978 (MADISON AND ESTILL COUNTIES)

UFO sightings in the South have often occurred in clusters over a particular city or state at a particular time. This is certainly the case with a number of UFO reports in the *National Enquirer* from Madison and Estill Counties in 1978. Their credibility is enhanced by the fact that some of these sightings were made by firemen and the police. For example, when the Madison County Fire Department was called to investigate a grass fire, they were surprised to find a saucer-shaped UFO that was "blazing red" in color. They chased the strange craft for over an hour across Richmond. The police were involved in a UFO sighting in Estill County. On February 19, 1978, Kentucky state trooper Jim Whitaker was driving along a country road when he saw a "car-shaped" object floating over a field. He noted that it had white, green, blue and red flashing lights. During his two-hour pursuit of the UFO, Whitaker noticed that the lights dimmed when an airplane or helicopter came near it but brightened up again in a clear sky.

Police Chief Marcus Cole reported that many people living in Irvine saw flying saucers in 1978. Newspaper publisher Guy Hatfield said that the

In 1978, Terry Kirby of Irvine saw an oval-shaped object like the one pictured here hovering over him while he was chopping wood. *Courtesy of Wikimedia Commons.*

eyewitnesses "were all solid citizens, with no reason to say it unless they saw one." One of these reports was made by Elmer Hardy, a seventy-three-year-old Methodist minister. He said that he and his wife were driving to church Sunday night when they saw a huge flying object appear out of the darkness and float over their car: "It was about 16 stories high and 20 stories wide, with a zillion lights on it." Another sighting in Irvine came from a much younger witness. Sixteen-year-old Terry Kirby said that he was chopping wood in the backyard when, suddenly, an oval-shaped object hovered over him. He described it as being "as big as a house." Fortunately, he had the presence of mind to dash inside the house and grab his Polaroid camera. One of his photographs was published in the *National Enquirer*.

The Kentucky UFO sightings of 1978 have been dismissed by many people because the story appeared in a tabloid with a questionable reputation. However, eyewitnesses living in Madison and Estill Counties still have vivid memories of what they saw. They take seriously the saying, "The truth is out there."

THE HOPKINSVILLE GOBLIN INCIDENT (HOPKINSVILLE)

One of America's most famous encounters with extraterrestrials took place on August 21, 1955, at the Sutton family home in Kelly, Kentucky, near Hopkinsville. According to the report the Suttons filed at the Hopkinsville police station that night, one of their friends, Billy Ray Taylor, had just filled a bucket with water from the well at 7:00 p.m. when what he described as a silver aircraft "real bright, and with exhaust all the colors of the rainbow" flew over the house, paused in the air and descended to the ground. He rushed into the house and breathlessly recounted what he had just seen. At the time, fifty-year-old Lucky Sutton and their wives, as well as a brother-in-law, were inside the house. The Sutton family did not take Billy Ray's story very seriously until one of the grown sons, Lucky Sutton, went to the back door and saw a creature three and a half feet tall with "an oversized head…almost perfectly round, [its] arms extended almost to the ground, [its] hands had talons…and [its oversized] eyes glowed with a yellowish light." They also observed that the creature seemed to be enveloped in a "shimmering light."

The two men immediately grabbed their weapons—a .22-caliber rifle and a 20-guage shotgun—and began shooting at the small humanoid standing in front of them. The creature flipped over and ran off. A few moments later, another creature appeared in a side window. Not even pausing to raise the window screen, the men fired repeatedly. Once again, the little being flipped over and vanished in the darkness. Mrs. Lankford, who was crouched on the floor next to Billy Ray during the gunfire, said, "It looked like a five-gallon gasoline can with a head on top and small legs. It was a shimmering bright metal, like on my refrigerator."

Driven by curiosity, Billy Ray opened the door and cautiously ventured outside. He was standing under a small overhanging roof when a claw-like appendage reached down and touched his hair. Several family members yelled at him and dragged him back inside the house. Lucky ran outside and fired his gun at the roof and at one of the "things" in a tree. Seemingly unfazed by the gunfire, the creature flew to the ground and vanished.

For the next several hours, the family huddled inside the house, listening to the scratching sounds on the roof. Finally, at 11:00 p.m., they mustered up enough courage to dash to their cars and drive as fast as they could to the police station. They convinced the police chief that they had really been attacked by something from another planet. A few minutes later, several local policemen, accompanied by members of the state police and the military police from Fort Campbell, converged on the Sutton farm. They were unable to find any evidence of a violent attack except for a large number of shell casings scattered on the ground and on the floor of the house. Thinking that the aliens might have been conjured up by a long night of partying, the officers searched the house but were unable to find any liquor bottles or cans of beer. The Suttons went to bed, only to have their slumber disturbed at 2:30 a.m. by the reappearance of one of their night visitors. Mrs. Lankford claimed that she saw the claws of one of the family's glowing assailants on the window screen by her bed.

Not surprisingly, the UFO incident generated a huge amount of interest in the media. For the next few days, reporters from radio stations and newspapers in Kentucky descended on the little family farm. Even the *New York Times* carried the story of the "Hopkinsville Goblins." The press's reference to the creatures as "Little Green Men" in their news stories was the first time the term had been used in the media. Unable to deter curiosity seekers from invading their privacy, the Suttons decided to cash in on their home's notoriety, charging fifty cents admission to the grounds, one dollar for information and ten dollars for photographs. Naturally, the family's profiting from the incident led to accusations in the press that they had invented the whole story.

However, not all of the Suttons' visitors following their ordeal were unwelcome. Local radio reporter Bud Ledwith talked to the family several days later and made drawings of the creatures based on their descriptions. He was struck by the consistency of their memories of the appearance of the little aliens. In 1956, UFOlogist Isabel Davis conducted several interviews with the Suttons. Her investigation resulted in a two-hundred-page report including interviews, drawings and maps. She was convinced in the end that the Suttons had not perpetrated an elaborate hoax on the community at large. Mrs. Lankford impressed Davis as a very honest, serious-minded person who disliked being in the public eye.

Skeptics believe that the "aliens" that attacked the Sutton family home in Hopkinsville in 1955 was actually a flock of great horned owls. *Courtesy of Wikimedia Commons.*

In 2006, a member of the Committee for Skeptical Inquiry conducted his own investigation of the incident. He noted right away that the large number of reports of a UFO in the area that night suggested the possibility that a meteor might have made its way to earth. He also believed that the "little green men" who tormented the Sutton family were actually great horned owls, whose long wings and talons could resemble arms and clawed hands under the right conditions. Their shimmery appearance could have been produced by the moonlight glimmering on their feathers and talons.

The logical explanations for the "alien attack" at the Sutton farm has not lessened the allure of the legend. For over sixty years, the Little Green Men Festival has been held at Hopkinsville and Kelly. The two-day event features live music, an alien costume contest and a thirty-eight-foot-wide "UFO." Authors of books and articles on the incident hold book signings at the festival and show up for book signings. No longer is Hopkinsville known solely as the birthplace of seer Edgar Cayce.

Chapter 8

MYSTERIOUS DEATHS

Octavia Hatcher (Pikesville)

Burials in nineteenth-century America did not always signal the end of life. In 1822, a forty-year-old German shoemaker who seemed to be dead was placed in a coffin and buried, even though his body displayed no signs of rigor mortis. As the gravedigger was shoveling the last clods of dirt on the grave, he heard a knocking sound from way under the ground. Frantically, the grave digger dug up the coffin and pulled the shoemaker out. Unfortunately, he died three days later. In 1915, thirty-year-old Essie Dunbar from South Carolina died from a severe attack of epilepsy. However, the doctors' original diagnosis was reversed after her sister had the body exhumed. When the lid was opened, Essie sat up and smiled. Another classic example of premature burial occurred in Kentucky.

Octavia Smith was born in Pikesville, Kentucky, on May 21, 1870, to Jacob and Pricey Smith. Her father, who owned a dry-goods business, was one of the founders of Pikesville. Because she came from a prominent family, Octavia was viewed as a suitable match for James Hatcher, one of the wealthiest men in town. His business ventures began when he opened a warehouse on the river at the age of eighteen. Following the ill-advised investment in the construction of a steamer, Hatcher became a successful contractor. In 1886, he built the Pikesville Courthouse. Hatcher's fortunes improved considerably after he entered the timber business. With the money he earned from the sale of timber, Hatcher invested in land and founded the James Hatcher Coal Company. When he married Octavia Smith in 1889, the future looked bright for both of them.

Unfortunately, the Hatchers' marital bliss was short-lived. In January 1891, Octavia gave birth to a son, Jacob, who died shortly thereafter. Octavia sank into such a deep depression that she seemed to lack the will to live. She eventually became gravely ill and slipped into a coma in April. On May 2, doctors pronounced her dead from an unknown illness. The unseasonably high temperatures, combined with the fact that she was not embalmed, led to the decision to bury her quickly in the Hatcher family plot.

James Hatcher was still reeling from the loss of his wife and son when he received word several days later that other residents of Pikesville were afflicted with some sort of sleeping sickness after being bitten by a fly. Alarmed at the prospect of having accidentally buried his wife alive, James quickly arranged for her body to be exhumed. The sight that greeted the family's eyes when the lid of the coffin was opened filled them with horror. Octavia's face was contorted in agony. A closer examination revealed that her fingernails were bloodied and broken, and the silk covering on the coffin's lid was ripped to shreds. The shock she must have felt when she realized her predicament must have been unimaginable. Octavia Hatcher was reburied with a statue of her likeness perched on top of an expensive monument. Years later, vandals broke off the small statue of a baby cradled in his mother's arm.

The legend of Octavia Hatcher's two burials evolved considerably over the years. In the most commonly told variant, Octavia was pregnant when she died. After she died, people passing by her grave heard the crying of a baby. When her husband exhumed the coffin, he was surprised to find that his infant son was alive, even though his mother had died. The baby followed her mother in death shortly thereafter. In recent years, teenagers and college students who ventured out to the cemetery swore that Octavia Hatcher's statue moved. Youthful trespassers generated another apocryphal tale about Octavia's statue. They said that because of Octavia's indignation at being buried alive, her statue occasionally turned away from Pikesville and faced the other direction. The credibility of this variant disappeared after the authorities learned that teenagers had climbed on top of the monument and turned the statue around. Not all of the stories about Octavia Hatcher's ghost can be dismissed this easily. Neighbors living near the cemetery have heard the disturbing sound of weeping coming from there. When they approach Octavia Hatcher's grave, the weeping abruptly ceases.

WHAT HAPPENED TO NANCY DADDYSMAN?
(BOWLING GREEN)

Prior to moving to Bowling Green in 1998, forty-two-year-old Nancy Daddysman worked at a Glasgow nursing home. When she was hired, she was living in the Star Motel in Cave City. By September, she was living at 1050 Shive Lane in Bowling Green. On September 4, 1998, her car broke down in town. She was wearing red jeans, a white shirt and white tennis shoes. A friend of hers dropped her off at the local Waffle House on Three Springs Road to meet her friends. She told them she was going to call a friend of hers and ask him to drive her to Indianapolis. She left the restaurant and was never seen again. Shirley Clancy, her mother, reported Nancy missing. No one knows the identity of the person who was going to give her a ride.

Her disappearance remained a mystery until September 21, 2009, when two teenagers who were cave diving discovered skeletal remains in a roadside dump off Iron Mountain Road near Park City. The closest building was a Baptist church. The corpse was wrapped in a blanket. An autopsy revealed that she had been stabbed to death. Detective Rusty Anderson said that her murderer had attempted to conceal the body. Her body had apparently not been moved in the two years since it had been buried. Forensic anthropologist Dr. Emily Crain identified the corpse as being that of Nancy Daddysman. Investigators believed that her killer was probably someone who was familiar with the heavily wooded area. Nancy's murder was featured in an episode of the television show *Unsolved Mysteries* in 2001.

The identity of her killer proved to be elusive. Nancy's friend Jack Woodbine was eliminated early on as a subject, as were her family members. Her ex-husband could not have murdered her, because he was living at a military base in Langley, Virginia, when she vanished. For eight years, the investigation reached one dead end after another. Her death appeared to be a motiveless crime. She had no enemies as far as anyone knew. Then, in 1990, David M. Bell confessed to the murder of Nancy Daddysman and several other people. He told authorities that he picked up Nancy while she was hitchhiking. They were on their way to Indianapolis when he began striking her repeatedly with an iron pipe. She surprised him by fighting back. Bell was only able to subdue her by stabbing her repeatedly with a knife. He admitted to authorities that he was under the influence of methamphetamine at the time. Bell buried her body in a shallow grave at the roadside dump and drove off. His story was verified by a defensive wound on Nancy's arm. After a series of interviews with Bell, investigators concluded that he was a serial killer who had murdered over seventeen women, including his mother, whom he electrocuted in a bathtub in 1991. Bell is now serving a sixty-five-year sentence for the murder of Claire Ellis. At the time of this writing, Bell has not been tried for the murder of Nancy Daddysman.

Who Was "Tent Girl"? (Lexington)

On May 17, 1968, Wilbur Riddle was walking along US Route 25 near Georgetown, Kentucky, looking for glass insulators, when he found the badly decomposed nude body of a woman who appeared to be between sixteen and nineteen years old. The corpse was wrapped in heavy green canvas tarpaulin, the type of fabric used to make large tents. Identifying the body was complicated by the lack of dental work. Investigators publicized a sketch of what the young woman might have looked like and general information about her height, weight and hair color. After a while, the case went cold. She was buried in 1971 in the Georgetown Cemetery. The inscription on the tombstone identified the young woman as "Tent Girl."

The case remained unsolved until 1998. Twenty-seven-year-old Todd Matthews of Livingston, Tennessee, became interested in the Tent Girl mystery after marrying one of Wilbur Riddle's daughters. Even three decades after finding the girl's body, Riddle was haunted by the mystery of who she was and what had happened to her. Matthews began reading through reports of missing persons on the Internet. In 1997, he created his own website for the case in the hopes that someone would come forward with useful information. Combing through hundreds of reports finally paid off in 1998, when he found a description of a young married woman posted by the Hackman family on a missing person's website. She had turned up missing in Lexington in 1967. Matthews emailed the information from the Tent Girl's police report to the person who was listed on the website as a contact for the family: Rosemary Westbrook of Benton, Arkansas. Excited by the possibility that Tent Girl might be her missing sister, Rosemary contacted the Scott County Sheriff's Office. Rosemary's description of her sister's facial features, such as a gap between her front teeth, matched the coroner's description of the body from 1968. The police exhumed the body for the purpose of collecting DNA evidence. On April 26, 1998, the sheriff's office formally identified the corpse known only as "Tent Girl" as being that of Barbara Ann Hackman, who had been married to a carnival worker named George Earl Taylor. She was twenty-four years old when she died. At the time of the announcement, Barbara's daughter was married and living in Ohio. Barbara's body was reburied in Georgetown Cemetery; her real name was added to the original gravestone. Her family omitted her married name from the inscription. Barbara's husband told the Hackman family that Barbara had run off with another man. This was the reason he gave for not turning in a missing person's report. Many people in the community believed that Taylor murdered his wife. He was never formally accused of the crime, however, because he died of cancer in October 1987. Her murder is still unsolved.

THE MYSTERY OF MOUNTAIN JANE DOE (HARLAN COUNTY)

On a hot day in June 1969, a man was picking flowers near Little Shepherd Trail in Harlan County when he found the body of a woman. She had clearly been stabbed to death. Investigators determined that she was in her late teens or early twenties and that she had been stabbed multiple times. The Harlan County Rescue Squad transported the unknown young woman to the hillside paupers' cemetery. Local residents arranged for a funeral; they donated flowers as well.

For forty years, the identity of the girl known only as "Mountain Jane Doe" was unknown. In 2009, Karen Stipes initiated a search of the NamUS database for Sonja Kay Blair-Adams. Stipes was exploring the possibility that her mother was Mountain Jane Doe. Assisting her in this endeavor was Knox County, Tennessee cold-case detective Amy Dobbs, who collected DNA samples for the family. Five years later, mortuary owner Darla Jackson, coroner Philip Bianchi and the Kentucky State Police arranged for Jane Doe's body to be exhumed so that a DNA sample could be taken and matched with the DNA of the family members. However, because many of the grave markers in the cemetery were just pieces of aluminum, they realized later on that they had dug up the wrong body. The investigators returned in November 2009 and found Jane Doe's grave. In 2016, the Kentucky State Police issued a press release stating that DNA evidence positively identified Mountain Jane Doe as Sonja Kay Blair-Adams.

The burial of Sonja Kay Blair-Adams marked the end of the case. Willie DeHart, Blair-Adams's sister, said that she and her family took comfort in giving her a decent burial, but she added that, as far as they were concerned, the case was not closed. "Our next milestone will be finishing, finding who did it," DeHart said.

THE FACE IN THE CUPOLA WINDOW (RUSSELLVILLE)

The possibility that lightning could transfer the image of a face to a window has been a staple of American folklore from its colonial beginnings. This narrative is so common, in fact, that it is listed in Ernest Warren Baughman's *Type and Motif Index of the Folktales of England and North America* as "E531(a) "Ghost-like portrait etched in glass." The best known of these legends in the Deep South is probably the face of Henry Wells in the garret window of the Pickens County Courthouse in Carrollton, Alabama. However, Russellville, Kentucky, has a lesser known but equally intriguing "face in the window" legend.

The site of the fabled window is the Sexton House at 515 West Ninth Street, across from the northeast corner of Maple Grove Cemetery. The Victorian-era home was built in 1870. In all of the variants of the legend, the caretaker's daughter was standing in the cupola on a "dark and stormy night" when, in a fit of anger, she cursed God. A few seconds later, she was struck by lightning, and her image was preserved in one of the windows from the storm itself, which ruined the picnic that she and her boyfriend had planned. In another version, she flew into a rage after her parents forbade her to go to a dance with the boy. Of course, none of these variants takes into account the likelihood that the young woman died from natural causes, such as an illness, probably because this scenario is much less sensational. The image itself varies, as well. In some variants, only her face is imprinted on the glass; in others, the nude image of her entire body appears in the window, because she was bathing when she found out that she could not rendezvous with her boyfriend. As word of the phenomenon spread through the state, so many people drove by the Sexton House that in the 1920s the owners decided to paint over the window. In several versions, a caretaker named Kelly Williamson attempted to remove the paint but suffered a heart attack in the kitchen before he finished. In another version, the man simply gave up.

Legend has it that a flash of lightning created the image of the caretaker's daughter in the window of the Sexton House's cupola.

Like many legends involving children and young people, this one can be viewed as a cautionary tale. Some locals took the ghostly image as a warning to children against cursing God. Others believe that the woman was punished by the Lord for disobeying her parents. The mystery surrounding her death is deepened by the absence of the fabled image, which may or may not be hidden under the coat of paint on the window. The Sexton House is a private residence, so the only way to really see the window is from the graveyard.

THE BODY IN THE STORM DRAIN (FLORENCE)

Countless crimes would probably go undetected were it not for a chance discovery. Such was the case with a grisly find by two public works officers for the City of Florence on November 17, 2005. The men were cleaning a storm drain just off the southbound lane of I-75, not far from St. Elizabeth's

Hospital. One of the workers was raking up a pile of debris when he spotted what appeared to be a human skull. After a few minutes, the workers found the rest of the skeletal remains inside a pair of blue nylon overalls. An investigation conducted by the authorities concluded that the individual was probably a homeless man.

The police revised their original findings a few weeks later following an anthropological examination by Dr. Emily Craig. She concluded that the deceased was a Caucasian male between forty-five and sixty-five years old who had had open-heart surgery. Previous injuries to the ribs, head and nose were clearly visible. More clues to the man's identity took the form of a movie-club membership card and a hotel key card in the pockets of the overalls. Through sheer luck, DNA evidence was preserved in several cigarette butts found in a nest mice had made inside the skull. The investigators also noticed that the man's name patch had been cut off, leading them to believe that he was the victim of foul play. Unfortunately, the hotel key card did not match any current records. A sharp-eyed investigator spotted blood on the card, but it was too degraded to be of any use.

When news of the discovery of the skeletal remains was broadcast in the local media, the police department was flooded with phone calls from people seeking information about the man in the hope that he might be their missing loved one. The police finally got a break when Florence Police detective Walt Colley uncovered a missing person's report about a sixty-five-year-old Alzheimer's patient named Otha Young Jr. from Louisville who had signed himself out of the hospital where his family had placed him for treatment and driven off in his car, a Ford, on October 9, 1996. Using sample tissue taken from Young at the time of his surgery, the investigators were able to match his DNA with that found on the skeletal remains in October 2005. Although Otha Young Jr.'s family has received closure, of a sort, his loved ones cannot rest until his killer has been brought to justice.

Chapter 9

MYSTERIOUS MONSTERS

The Lake Herrington Monster
(Mercer, Garrard and Boyle Counties)

Lake Herrington was created in 1925 when a dam was constructed on the Dix River for the purpose of generating hydroelectric power. Covering nearly four miles, Lake Herrington is a prime fishing destination with an abundance of bluegill, catfish, crappie and bass. However, the most famous denizen of the deepest lake in Kentucky cannot be found in any taxonomy.

The Lake Herrington Monster is referred to by locals as "Herry" or the "Eel-Pig" because of its strange appearance. It is best described as a hybrid of an eel and a pig with a snout and a curly tail. According to witnesses, the fifteen-foot-long creature's skin has speckled mottling. Its streamlined body enables it to swim as fast as a motorboat.

Tales of a terrifying lake monster date to the 1920s. Rumors of a pig-like monster began circulating after a couple of dogs dragged the head of a pig out of the water. The first authoritative sighting of Herry was reported by Professor Lawrence S. Thompson in the *Louisville Courier* in August 1972. In the interview, Thompson said that he had seen the creature several times from his lake house. He theorized that generations of the beast's ancestors had been living in a cave totally undisturbed until it was submerged during the construction of Dix Dam.

In November 2006, a fisherman described his encounter with Herry on the website Fishin.com. In 1977, he was fishing from a boat with his uncle and his uncle's best friend at Chimney Rock when a strange creature broke the surface of the water near the boat. He recalled that the manatee-like cryptid was three feet wide and longer than the boat. After ten minutes, it vanished beneath the surface of the water. They were unable to catch a glimpse of the monster's head and tail. The men were so startled by the sudden appearance of their aquatic visitor that they forgot about the camera they had taken with them. Their frustration escalated when they realized that they had missed an opportunity to release the Lake Herrington Monster from the realm of myth.

THE DEMON LEAPER (LOUISVILLE)

Tales of flying human-like creatures can be found in folk traditions throughout the world. The Yakama tribe in Washington State told of the Lechuza, a race of cannibalistic owl-women who lived in caves and fed on the flesh of children. In the twentieth and twenty-first centuries, reports of these creatures spread to Texas and Mexico. Victorian England produced its own version of a menacing phantom. In 1837, the residents of London reported answering their door, only to be attacked by a devilish figure that raked their clothes with its claws and then leaped away. Stories of the strange figure known as Spring-Heeled Jack peaked in 1838 and then faded away. At the turn of the twentieth century, a similar creature paid a visit to Old Louisville.

In the 1880s, articles published in the *Courier Journal* and the *Madisonville Times* reported a shiny creature being seen jumping from the rooftops of buildings in downtown Louisville. Some witnesses described him as wearing a shiny suit; others said that he had shiny skin. Other people said that it was a bat-like creature with leathery skin, wings and talons. A few people swore that they had been poked and scratched by the creature. On September 12, 1880, the *New York Times* published an article about the Louisville monster sightings, "An Aerial Mystery." The article reported the appearance of a similar creature near Coney Island. Witnesses described it as "a man with bat's wings and improved frog's legs." After the Walnut Street Baptist Church was built in 1902 in Louisville, some people noted similarity between the gargoyles peering down from the church and the

A flying humanoid creature called the "Demon Leaper" perched on top of the Walnut Street Baptist Church.

Demon Leaper. Not surprisingly, many people claimed to have seen the Demon Leaper on the roof of the Walnut Street Baptist Church.

Louisville's Demon Leaper was the country's most famous humanoid winged creature until the appearance of the Moth Man in Point Pleasant, West Virginia, from November 15, 1966, to December 15, 1967. In the book *The Mystery Chronicles: More Real-Life X-Files*, author Joe Nickell suggests that the creature misidentified as the Moth Man was actually a barn owl. One wonders if Louisville's Demon Leaper might also have its real-life counterpart in the natural world.

KENTUCKY'S GIANT HUMAN SKELETONS (PINE GROVE)

Tales of giants have been around almost since the beginning of civilization. In ancient Greek myth, giants were the children of Uranus (the Sky) and Gaia (the Earth). According to Greek historian Solinus, a battle was fought between the gods and a race of giants, who were defeated and buried under mountains. Giants are also an important part of Judeo-Christian beliefs. In the biblical book of Samuel, the shepherd boy David slays a Philistine giant, Goliath, in armed combat. History also records the existence of giants. The tallest person in history, Robert Wadlow (February 22, 1918– July 15, 1940), lived in Alton, Illinois. In the eighteenth, nineteenth and early twentieth centuries, evidence of the existence of giants was found in Kentucky as well.

In his book *Historical Sketches of Kentucky*, Kentucky historian Lewis Collins recounts the discovery of giant human bones at Augusta, Kentucky, near the Ohio River, by John Payne in 1792. Payne found a number of large human skeletons and dozens of scattered bones within a range of a mile and a half. The largest skeletons were seven feet tall. He also dug up ten giant skeletons in the cellar of his house.

Collin reported that giant bones were excavated in Hardin County in 1850 around Rolling Fork. One of the thigh bones was estimated to be six times the size of the thigh bone of an average modern human, making the owner around twelve or thirteen feet tall. Eight years later, oversized human bones were excavated in an Indian mound in Adair County.

The November 24, 1911 edition of the *Cincinnati Enquirer* published an intriguing article, "Sepulcher Containing the Skeletons of Prehistoric Giants Is Unearthed in Kentucky." According to the reporter, a wealthy farmer

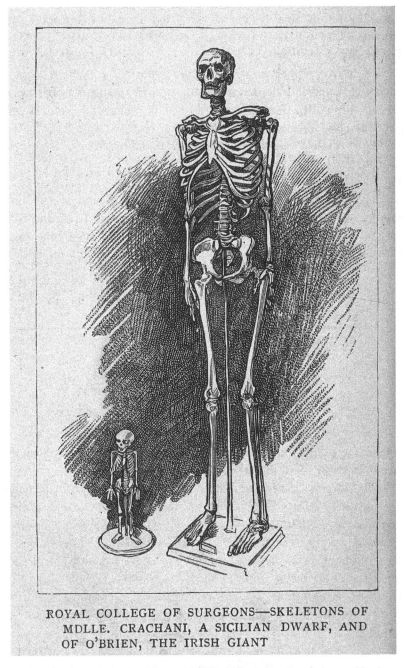

ROYAL COLLEGE OF SURGEONS—SKELETONS OF
MDLLE. CRACHANI, A SICILIAN DWARF, AND
OF O'BRIEN, THE IRISH GIANT

In 1911, newspapers reported that a sepulcher containing giant skeletons, like that of O'Brien the Irish Giant, was discovered in Kentucky.

named Hugh Yates was digging under a high cliff on his property when he discovered a large grave containing several oversized human skeletons: "His curiosity aroused, Mr. Yates called in some neighbors, and, armed with picks, they burrowed their way into the side of the cliff and found an ancient sepulcher crowded with human skeletons, some of them larger than the one first found. One of the frames measured 12 feet." The writer went on to say that the men also uncovered jewelry, cooking vessels, strange ornaments and a number of musical instruments. He ended by stating that the diggers were continuing to excavate the site.

The most recent discovery of giant bones took place in Breathitt County in 1965. While erecting cattle stalls near a stone foundation, Kenneth White discovered a skeleton eight feet, nine inches tall. Upon inspection, he observed some intriguing deviations from the physiology of the average human being. The feet were small in relation to the rest of the body, the eye and nose sockets were slits and the jaw hinges were solid bone, making speech difficult. Folklorist Michael Henson said that the bones were reburied without being photographed.

KENTUCKY'S DEVIL MONKEYS (ALBANY)

Devil Monkeys have been a staple of southern folklore for decades. The first reported sighting of a simian-like beast occurred in South Pittsburgh, Tennessee, in 1934. However, the first "official" Devil Monkey sighting occurred in 1959. Mr. and Mrs. Boyd were driving through the mountains in Saltville, Virginia, when their car was attacked by a beast with definite ape-like features. Most of the later eyewitnesses described the creatures as having large teeth, pronounced musculature, strong legs, white hair around the stomach and neck and a prominent nose. Most eyewitnesses describe them as standing between three and four feet tall, although a few people have estimated the height to be as much as seven feet. People also say that Devil Monkeys have three toes, razor-sharp claws and bushy tails. The face is canine-like, similar to a baboon's. Encounters with the creatures have also occurred in the Midwest and Alaska.

Devil Monkey sightings in Kentucky date to the 1930s, but the most famous occurred in 1973. Cryptozoologist Loren Coleman traveled to Albany, Kentucky, to investigate reports of the slaughter of livestock by three large, black ape creatures with bushy tails. Afterward, Coleman wrote, "I investigated that case in depth. I interviewed the people, who were very sincere. In the whole context of devil monkey reports, it seemed extremely sincere."

One of the most recent sightings occurred on August 1, 2018, near Mammoth Cave National Park in Edmonson County. A man identified on the Pine Barrens Institute website only as "Rocky" said that he was driving home on Highway 728 when he saw a white creature with powerful legs standing between six and seven and a half feet tall on the left side of the road. Its pinkish face seemed to be frozen in a snarl, giving it a very menacing look.

THE POPE LICK MONSTER (LOUISVILLE)

Urban legends are contemporary tales, supposedly based on fact, that contain elements of horror, humor and the supernatural. Proving their veracity is often the reason behind legend tripping, which involves nocturnal pilgrimages to the sites of horrific, tragic or supernatural events. In many communities, these sojourns are taken by adolescents, many of whom are also motivated by the desire to prove their courage and to party in a remote area beyond the scrutiny of authority figures. One of Kentucky's best-known legend-tripping destinations is the Pope train trestle, the home of the Pope Lick Monster, in the Fisherville area just outside of Louisville,

The Pope Lick Monster is said to be a hybrid of a human being and a goat or, in some variants, a sheep. The monster lives under the Southern Railroad trestle spanning Floyd's Fork Creek. Built in the late 1880s, the rusted trestle spans a distance of 772 feet. The absence of rails makes it particularly dangerous for anyone foolhardy enough to walk out on it. The beast is usually described as having long, greasy hair on its head and legs and pointed horns protruding from its forehead. In the standard version of the creature's backstory, the goat man is a circus freak who vents its resentment at being mistreated on anyone who passes by the bridge. In one of the variants, the freakish beast fled from a train that derailed on the trestle. In an entirely different version, a farmer who sacrificed goats to Satan was transformed into a goat man.

Adding to the danger posed by the legend's treacherous setting is the goat man's hatred for trespassers who scale the eight-foot bridge surrounding the base of the trestle. The creature is said to have the ability to hypnotize its victims just before the arrival of an oncoming train. Some locals believe that

A hybrid monster called the "Goat Man" is said to live under the Pope Lick Bridge.

the creature uses voice mimicry to draw teenagers into the path of the train. Others say that it jumps onto the roofs of cars passing under the trestle.

The fact that no one has actually seen the Pope Lick Monster has not discouraged thrill seekers from venturing out to the Pope Lick Bridge at night. A fence was erected because of the deaths that have occurred at the bridge. One of these tragic accidents happened on April 23, 2016. Ignoring the "No Trespassing" sign, twenty-six-year-old Roquel Bain and her boyfriend, David Knee, climbed onto the bridge to take a photograph of a train. They were standing on the bridge when a train appeared forty feet in front of them. David jumped off the side of the bridge and gripped its metal edge with both arms and one of his legs. Roquel was not so lucky. She was struck by the train so hard that her body flew through the air before hitting the ground ninety feet below. In an interview with reporter Beth Warren, David Knee said, "My life is basically destroyed; I'm mentally crushed," This particular incident proves that the dangers of legend tripping can be very real indeed.

THE HILLBILLY BEAST (KENTUCKY)

According to the Kentucky Bigfoot Research organization, over four hundred sightings of the monster have been reported in the state since the late eighteenth century. Evidence of the earliest sightings takes the form of prehistoric artwork. A rock painting of a humanoid-like creature with a feline muzzle and ears was found at Asphalt Rock. According to a timeline in Michael Newton's *Strange Kentucky Monsters*, the earliest sighting of a Bigfoot by a White settler was frontiersman Daniel Boone's. He claimed to have shot and killed a hairy, ten-foot-tall monster that he called a "Yahoo" in the late 1770s. Over fifty years later, an article in the October 24, 1878 edition of the *Louisville Courier Journal* reported that a "wild man" standing six feet, seven inches tall was captured in Tennessee and featured in a sideshow in Louisville. Unlike the typical specimens, however, this one was covered with a layer of scales. In 1894, the residents of Washington chased a large "man-beast" that was stealing chickens. Supposedly, it was wearing a sheepskin loincloth.

A larger number of Bigfoot sightings were reported in the twentieth century. In 1907, a farmer in Garrard County witnessed a very hairy man chasing a dog. Trackers found human-like handprints on the ground, leading them to conclude that the "monster" may have been an "escaped lunatic." In the 1930s, Rowan County residents Charles Nickell and his family became terrified when an ape-like beast tried to break into their home. In April 1944, a man was fishing in the Big Sandy River when he was accosted by a large, hairy creature that grabbed his catch and lumbered off into the forest.

The number of Bigfoot sightings in Kentucky increased dramatically in the second half of the twentieth century. In 1957, a woman named Phyllis and two relatives were driving down a back road in Lee County when a huge, dark figure stepped in front of their car, blocking their way. Their attacker proceeded to toss large tree branches at the family's vehicle for over twenty minutes before Phyllis finally decided to turn around and go back the way they had come. In the 1960s and '70s, dozens of individuals living in Henderson County complained to authorities that a huge creature was killing their livestock. The monster's size in the reports varied from eight to twelve feet. Twenty-seven sightings were reported in the 1980s, including that of a Bigfoot that chased a woman around her car in a shopping center in Maysville. One of the forty-three sightings in the 1990s was turned in by Harry Hopkins, who saw a Bigfoot standing in the south fork of the Cumberland River near Devil's Jump in McCreary County.

On July 27, 2019, a stranger informed a couple camping in the backwoods of Mammoth Cave National Park that he had had an encounter with Bigfoot.

By the beginning of the twenty-first century, the number of sightings in Kentucky showed no signs of abating. On January 14, 2001, a man who was identified only as "M.I." was driving along a patch of woods in Greenup County one night when he saw an eight-foot humanoid in the road. After the creature loped off into the darkness, M.I. photographed the beast's tracks. Unlike Daniel Boone, who offered no actual proof of the Yahoo's existence, today's eyewitnesses are using everyday technology to prove that Bigfoot is much more than the stuff of nightmares.

One of the most recent—and highly publicized—of Kentucky's Bigfoot sightings occurred in Mammoth Cave National Park on July 27, 2019. Madelyn Durand and Brad Ginn were asleep in their tent when they were awakened by a man and his young son. The couple could tell by the man's expression and the tone of his voice that he was clearly agitated. In a tremulous voice, he exclaimed that a Bigfoot-like creature had destroyed several tents in his campsite. Drawing a pistol from his back pocket, he admonished them to keep their eyes open and to yell if they heard or saw anything out of the ordinary. As he left, he assured the couple that he would rush to their aid if they needed him.

Completely baffled by the strange man's warning and erratic behavior, Madelyn and Brad tried to get back to sleep, but a few minutes later, at 2:00

a.m., the comforting silence of their surroundings was broken by several nearby gunshots. Later that morning, park rangers investigated the report and ascertained that neither man nor beast had been harmed during the night. Madelyn and Brad were particularly unnerved by the fact that their night visitor had fired in total darkness about twenty yards from their tent. A park ranger told them that firearms were permitted in the park but could not be discharged. The identity of the Bigfoot witness is still unknown.

Chapter 10

NATIVE AMERICAN LEGENDS

THE LEGENDS OF YAHOO FALLS
(DANIEL BOONE NATIONAL FOREST)

Cherokee storytellers have related two tales about Yahoo Falls. In one of these tales, a mixed-blood trader named Yahula lived in a stone house near the waterfall that bears his name. He often rode his horse on his trade routes through the hills and mountains, singing his favorite songs as a string of bells tinkled from the necks of his ponies. One day, he decided to taste the food of the little people, who were called the Nunehi, even though partaking of their delicacies was forbidden. When the Cherokee warriors returned from their hunt, they were surprised to find that Yahula had been taken to the Spirit World by the Nunehi. The Cherokee believe that one can still hear Yahula's spirit singing his songs to the tinkling of his ponies' bells at Yahoo Falls.

The second legend focuses on the massacre at Yahoo Falls. People say that in 1778, a young private in the Continental army named Jacob Troxell was dispatched to Post Vincennes to persuade the Cherokee to support Washington's army. While he was there, he befriended Tukaho Doublehead, the son of the principal chief of the Cherokee Nation, Taltsuska Doublehead. At the end of the American Revolution, Troxell married Princess Corn Blossom, one of the chief's four daughters. Jacob and Corn Blossom lived in a log cabin and herded cattle. The couple had a son named Little Jake. On January 15, 1810, Congress dismissed all of the Cherokees' land claims

Yahoo Falls in Daniel Boone National Forest is the site of the massacre of a band of Cherokee Indians on August 10, 1810. *Courtesy of Wikimedia Commons.*

in Kentucky and made plans to drive them out. In the summer of 1810, a Presbyterian minister named Blackburn offered protection to Cherokee women and children from the Cumberland Valley at the school he had opened near what is now Chattanooga. In early August, Corn Blossom told Little Jake to ride his horse to the neighboring villages and spread the word that the women and children would meet at the waterfall and depart from there to the Blackburn school. On August 10, 1810, Hiram Gregory's militia fired on the women and children as they began gathering at the rock shelter near the falls. More than one hundred women and children were massacred. Their bodies were interred in a high terrace behind the falls. The mass grave was undisturbed until the twentieth century, when loggers cut down the trees and rains washed the bones out of the hillside. Grave robbers scattered the bones and removed the artifacts. On January 31, 1811, Cherokee land was offered for sale at ten cents an acre.

The veracity of this story has been questioned for years by journalists and historians, who have found no contemporary accounts of the massacre itself or of the existence of Princess Corn Blossom. On August 12, 2006, an unofficial monument to the massacre was erected near the grave of Jacob Troxell without the permission of the National Forest Service. The forest service removed the monument because of the absence of any historical records indicating that the incident actually occurred.

THE DARK AND BLOODY GROUND (KENTUCKY)

The region that became Kentucky was known as "the dark and bloody ground" long before native inhabitants tried to drive the White settlers from their hunting grounds. The most likely source of the expression is the Cherokee chief Dragging Canoe, who signed the Treaty of Sycamore Shoals with Richard Henderson's Transylvania Company. The chief is reported to have said that a "dark cloud hung over the dark and bloody ground" because of the bad relations among the Cherokee, Shawnee and Iroquois. A different legend comes from the Delaware tribe. It relates that the Lenni-Lenape tribe

This chainsaw stump carving of a family of Cherokee Indians can be found in Big Springs Park in Versailles, Kentucky. *Courtesy of Wikimedia Commons.*

from the North and West allied with the Iroquois to exterminate the Allegwi people, who first laid claim to the land. Afterward, all of the tribes viewed the land, Kenhtake, as cursed, because it was a dark and bloody ground. Colonial land speculators preferred Dragging Canoe's version, asserting that if the region did not belong to any particular tribe, then the Indians' hunting grounds were free for the taking by any White settlers who wanted to live there—the implication being that Indians had never lived in the region that we now call Kentucky.

THE MOON-EYED PEOPLE (KENTUCKY)

The Cherokee oral tradition of the Moon-Eyed People first appeared in print in Benjamin Smith Barton's book *New Views of the Origin of the Tribes and Nations of America* (1797). One of his sources, Colonel Leonard Marbury, told Barton that the Moon-Eyed People of the Cherokee could not see well in daylight. In his 1902 publication *Myths of the Cherokee*, James Mooney wrote of an ancient race of White people, small in stature, who were driven out by the Cherokee. These White men, known as the Moon-Eyed People, had beards and blue eyes. They spent most of the daylight hours in their houses of logs and mud, because the sunlight hurt their eyes. Unlike the Spanish explorers, the Moon-Eyed People were not infected with the lust for gold. They devoted most of their time building their stone fortifications and mounds in the mountains and valleys of Appalachia.

Some scholars have found a connection between the Moon-Eyed People and the legends of the Welsh Indians. These stories make reference to the fabled expedition led by Prince Madoc of Wales to America in 1170, predating Columbus's voyage by over three centuries. Because of the lack of substantial evidence, many historians dismiss this story as nothing more than a legend. Barbara Alice Mann, a scholar of Seneca descent, offered a different theory regarding the true identity of the Moon-Eyed People. She asserted that they were descendants of the Adena peoples, a collection of Native American tribes that lived in Appalachia between 100 and 200 BC. The Adena may have been the culture responsible for building the long, irregular wall at Fort Mountain State Park. Dr. Mann theorized that the Cherokee absorbed the Adena culture around 200 BC.

THE LITTLE PEOPLE (KENTUCKY)

In an article that appeared in the October–December 1946 issue of the *Journal of American Folklore*, authors John Witthoft and Wendell S. Haddock asserted that the Little People of the Cherokee is "a highly elaborated tradition in which European motifs are rare." In other words, the legends of the Cherokee Little People were not carbon copies of the Leprechaun legends of Ireland and the fairy legends of German, English, Celtic and French cultures. Witthoft and Haddock did, however, find parallels in the dwarf lore of the Six Nations in North America.

One of the first written descriptions of the Little People of the Cherokee can be found in James Mooney's article "Myths of the Cherokee." He writes that they "hardly [reach] up to a man's knee but [are] well-shaped and handsome, with long hair falling almost to the ground." In his article "The Cherokee Legends of the Little People," David Farris cites the work of Betty J. Lombardi, who said that the Yunwi Tsunsdi, as the Little People were called, was a happy race that spent much of its time singing and dancing. They were capable of both kindness and fierce retribution. The Yunwi Tsunsdi helped people who showed them respect but punished anyone who gazed on them with either bad luck or death. Stories were told of cases in which Yunwi Tsunsdi helped people lost in the woods find their way back home, who then would lose their lives afterward when they told their friends and relatives about their encounter. In fact, the Cherokee considered it foolhardy to even utter the words *Yunwi Tsunsdi*, preferring instead to refer to them as *skill'li*, which means "ghost" or "witch." Some Cherokee claimed to have kept the Little People captive, in the belief that they would protect their home. Lombardi also suggested that the Little People were territorial, preferring to take the same path on their way to homes where people left food out for them.

Legend has it that the Little People even followed the Cherokee as they walked on the Trail of Tears. The Little People also kept the gift of eternal fire going as they made their way through snow and sleet. They were a great comfort to the Cherokee as they plodded along to their new home in Oklahoma.

Chapter 11

UNIVERSITY LEGENDS

UNION COLLEGE (BARBOURVILLE)

Union College was founded in 1879 by a group of thirty-five citizens who raised $20,000 to establish an institution of higher learning. The secretary of the first president named the school Union College to reflect the uniformity of the curriculum. In 1880, the college was moved from its temporary location over T. Gibson's store to a site provided by Thomas J. Wyatt. After the land was sold in 1886, the college was purchased by the Methodist church. The first AB degrees were conferred on June 8, 1893. Union College was nearly bankrupted when lightning destroyed the administration building. Union College was accredited by the University of Kentucky in 1927 and by the Southern Association of Colleges and Secondary Schools in 1932.

For a small institution, Union College seems to have more than its share of haunted buildings, several of which are recounted in Heather Dole's article "Haunted Halls in Union College," which appeared in the October 31, 2007 edition of the *Times Tribune*. One of the college's haunted dormitories is Lakeside Hall. This particular story involves the ill-advised use of a Ouija board, which some believe can open a portal to the "other side," through which negative energy can enter our world. One fall night in 1994, several members of a fraternity were entertaining themselves with a Ouija board a few days before Halloween. After the session, the young men claimed to have made contact with a female entity named Milan. When strange events began occurring inside the fraternity house, the men blamed them on their new "guest." In 1995, several staff members were holding a meeting on the

Centennial Hall, one of the oldest buildings on the campus of Union College, has served as an administration building and as a classroom building. *Courtesy of Wikimedia Commons.*

first floor of the fraternity house when they were interrupted by the sound of disembodied footsteps and the slamming of doors on the third floor. When they walked upstairs to investigate, they noticed that a light inside Room 317 was flickering. They made a sweep of the rest of the building but found no trace of an intruder. A few days later, a fraternity member woke up and was startled to see the outline of a woman sitting on the far end of his bed. She vanished a few seconds later.

Speed Hall is one of three buildings on the campus of Union College that have been named to the National Register of Historic Places. Speed Hall served as a women's dormitory when it opened in the 1905–6 school year. One of the ghosts that haunts the building is the spirt of a young woman who was devastated after receiving the news that her father had died. She felt indebted to the kindly man who worked in the coal mines to provide her with the kind of education and life that he never had. She walked up the stairs to her room on the third floor and began packing for the trip back home. Overwhelmed by grief, the girl stopped packing and sat on the bed, sobbing. The next day, her body was found hanging from the rafters. For years, the third floor of Speed Hall has been used for storage. Nevertheless, an active presence seems to inhabit the space. Many times over the years, students have seen a light in the window of the room where the girl is believed to have committed suicide, even though the room was padlocked. The coordinator of student conduct and campus safety paid little attention to the tales of the spectral light in Speed Hall until he had his own ghostly experience there in 1999. To prove that there was no truth to the stories, he turned off the lights in the building, beginning with the first floor. By the time he had turned off all of the lights and walked down the stairs, the light was back on. Assuming that someone had turned it on while he was on the other floors, he walked to the middle of the floor. Suddenly, he turned around, and there, at the bottom of the stairs, was the figure of a girl wearing an old-fashioned dress. He recalled later that she was bathed in a kind of eerie glow. After she disappeared, he walked out of the building and met a female student who asked him if he was closing up the building. When he replied that he was, she pointed up to the third floor, where a light in one of the rooms was still on. Conceding defeat, he went home.

Pfeiffer Hall is believed to be haunted by two ghosts. The sad story behind the first haunting can be found in colleges and universities throughout the country. Years ago, a young woman was dating a young man whom she fell in love with after several months of dating. One day, he confessed to her that he did not feel the same way about her that she felt about him, and he broke off their relations. The heartbroken girl returned to her dorm and threw herself on her bed, crying. For several days, she locked herself in her room, cutting classes and missing meals. One night, she put an end to her suffering by slashing her wrists with a razor blade. It is said that at that moment, a cold wind wafted through the dormitory. Since then, a spine-tingling moaning has echoed through the building at night. One morning at 4:00 a.m., the campus safety officer was talking to two girls on the first floor when they heard someone running upstairs. The trio walked upstairs and went to the lounge, where the residential advisor was sitting. After they told her about hearing someone running on that floor, she replied that she had not heard anything. She added that other students had heard the phantom footsteps on that particular floor.

The second ghost that haunts Pfeiffer Hall is the spirit of an athlete named James Garner who played football and basketball in the 1960s. On October 30, 1963, the six-foot, four-inch student was shutting the window in his second-floor dorm room when he tripped and fell through the window. He plummeted to his death on the sidewalk below. To this day, students say that if someone opens the window in Garner's former room, Room 245, at midnight, his ghost will shut it.

WESTERN KENTUCKY UNIVERSITY (BOWLING GREEN)

Western Kentucky University was established as a normal school on March 21, 1906, on the site of the Southern Normal School. The institution was relocated to "The Hill" in downtown Bowling Green on February 4, 1911. The first president was Henry Hardin Cherry. It was renamed Western Kentucky State Normal School and Teachers College in 1992. After merging with a men's school, the institution changed its name to Western Kentucky State Teachers College in 1930. The college changed its name once again in 1948, this time to Western Kentucky State College. In 1963, the Bowling Green College of Commerce was acquired by Western Kentucky State College and converted into a separate college within Western Kentucky's structure. The institution acquired its present name—Western Kentucky University—on June 16, 1966. WKU has continued to expand over the years, with branch campuses in Elizabethtown–Fort Knox, Glasgow and Owensboro.

One of the most haunted buildings on campus is Van Meter Hall. When it was built in 1911, the structure was designed to resemble a Greek temple. The events that are believed to have spawned the resident ghost occurred before construction was completed. One story goes that the contractor noticed that the concrete he had recently poured was seeping into an underground cave. Fearing bankruptcy, he jumped into the concrete. Not long after the contractor's suicide, a worker fell from the scaffolding and died on the floor of the lobby. Others say that the worker crashed through the skylight while working in the lobby. In all of the versions, the poor man expires in a pool of his own blood. Students still speak of the bloodstain that resists all attempts to remove it. In addition, eerie blue lights have been known to appear during performances. Curtains are said to open and close on their own as well, much to the chagrin of the stage crew.

At least one of WKU's ghosts is a benign spirit. McLean Hall is named for the secretary of President Henry Hardin Cherry, Mattie McLean. Because she is believed to be a vigilant spirit who looks out for the residents of the coed dorm, she instills comfort, not fear, in students. For years, residents have said that her portrait smiles at anyone who stares at it for long. Nothing happened to me when I stared at the portrait, probably because I ran out of time—and patience.

Potter Hall, a former women's dorm that now serves as an administration building, is much scarier than McLean Hall. It is said to be haunted by the spirit of a student who hanged himself in the basement in 1977. His

Students say Van Meter Hall at Western Kentucky University is haunted by the ghost of a construction worker. *Courtesy of Wikimedia Commons.*

unquiet spirit makes its presence known through sound. Students and staff report hearing disembodied footsteps roaming the building at night. Reports of someone dropping change into vending machines in empty hallways are fairly common. Because the ghost seems to enjoy terrifying people by dropping pennies on the floor, students have christened it "Penny."

LINDSEY-WILSON COLLEGE (COLUMBIA)

Founded in 1907 as Lindsey-Wilson Training School, the institution is named after the nephew and stepson of Catherine Wilson of Louisville. She donated $6,000 for the construction of one of the first buildings, which later became the L.R. McDonald Administration Building. Phillips Hall, a women's dormitory, bears the name of another generous donor, Mrs. James Phillips. Mrs. Kizzie Russell, a third early patron of the school, contributed $1,000. In the beginning, the institution functioned as a training school for teachers. Frank E. Lewis, the first principal, was replaced by S.L. Frogge. P.D. Neilson and R.R. Moss were appointed to that position in 1908. Lindsey-Wilson College (LWC) began offering junior-college courses in 1823; it officially became a junior college in 1934, although it continued serving as a training school from 1933 to 1979. LWC experienced a building boom under the leadership of A.P. White. Beginning in 1932, LWC added a number of new buildings, including a dining room and a gymnasium. LWC survived the Great Depression, thanks in large part to President White. Following his death in 1943, Victor P. Henry was given the task of closing the school, but he kept it open for another four years by refusing to take a salary and by putting government surplus furniture in the classroom. President John B. Horton initiated a second building boom in 1954. By the time his tenure ended in 1971, he had added a science building, a student union building and two dormitories, Horton Hall and Parrott Hall. LWC became a four-year college in 1985. President John B. Begley, who served as president for the next twenty years, was responsible for the construction of several buildings, including the Biggers Sports Center and the J.L. Turner Leadership Center. Under the leadership of President William T. Luckey Jr., LWC received its largest cash award when James. R. and Helen Lee Fugitte committed $8.6 million to the school. At the time of this printing, LWC has a staff of 380 and a student body of 2,600.

Institutions of higher learning with dormitories tend to be hotbeds of ghost stories. LWC's most haunted site is Horton Hall, a men's resident hall located between the soccer field and the gym. According to the Haunted America website, most of the reports of paranormal activity center on the second floor, where dark figures have been seen sighted pulling off the ceiling tiles late at night. Over the years, a ritual of sorts has been generated by the residents. Anyone wishing to summon the dark ones has to be perfectly still in bed, presumably at night. If the shadow figures recognize the form of a human being on the bed, the silence is broken by a piercing scream. So far, a backstory for the student body has not appeared.

In his book *Ghosts across Kentucky*, folklorist William Lynwood Montell includes a tale told to Lonnie Bailey by Debby Szczapinski in 1983 about a different dorm haunting. Although the name of the dorm is not given, the fact that it is a women's dorm suggests that it is probably Phillips Hall. She said that in 1975, the second floor of the dorm was unfinished at the time. Szczapinski said that, one night, she heard someone dragging a body across the floor upstairs. Later on, when her roommate told her the room was empty, Szczapinski found it difficult to curb her sense of unease. She believed that her encounter was connected somehow to the legend of a girl who hanged herself in the room years before when she learned that she was pregnant. Szczapinski's roommate had an even stranger experience with the occupant of the "empty" room upstairs. One night, she and the dorm mother walked up the stairs to the second floor to investigate a noise coming from one of the rooms. Szczapinski's roommate said that when she tried to open the door, it felt like someone was pulling on it from the inside. Szczapinski said that her roommate then got down on her hands and knees and peered under the door. To her amazement, she saw a green mist floating above the floor. Most likely, this was the same mist that she had heard students speak of. No feet were visible through the mist. In desperation—and fear—the dorm mother pulled out a gun and fired through the door. It slowly opened, and the pair entered the room. Nothing human or inhuman was present in the room.

MURRAY STATE UNIVERSITY (MURRAY)

Murray State Normal School was one of two teachers' colleges established by the General Assembly of the Commonwealth of Kentucky in the early twentieth century. Rainey T. Wells was largely responsible for convincing the Normal School Commission that Murray was an ideal location for one of the two schools. On November 26, 1922, the State Board of Education selected John Wesley Carr the first president of Murray State Normal School, despite the protests of the Normal School Commission, which believed that it had the power to choose Rainey T. Wells as president. The school opened its doors on September 23, 1923. Because none of the buildings had been constructed, the first classes were held on the first floor of Murray High School. Students either lived at home or boarded with local families. Wells Hall, the first building, was completed in 1925. Wilson Hall was built shortly before the end of Carr's three-year tenure as president. After Rainey T. Wells became the school's second president, several other buildings were completed, including the Carr Health Building, Pogue Library and Lovett Auditorium. The same year, the school received a new name, Murray State Normal School and Teachers College, and was designated a four-year institution with the authority to confer baccalaureate degrees. The Southern Association of Colleges and Schools accredited the institution in 1928. After the name was changed to Murray State Teachers' College in 1930, it was granted the power to offer pre-professional and liberal arts courses. When the name was changed to Murray State College in 1948, the administration added graduate-level courses. In 1966, the school became Murray State University in recognition of its expanded curriculum.

The students of Murray State University take pride in its traditions. For example, since 1965, students who get married have nailed their shoes to the "shoe tree." Since 1958, student organizations have competed in the All Campus Sing. Storytelling is an informal tradition that has been going on since the school's inception, especially the telling of ghost stories, a favorite pastime in colleges and universities across the country. One of the most haunted buildings on campus is the Sigma Epsilon House. In the 1970s, the fraternity rented rooms in "Ma" Crawford's boardinghouse after their fraternity house burned down. The bond between the brothers and Ma Crawford was so strong that they inherited her home after she died. For years, she has made her presence known to the fraternity members by turning the light in her former bedroom off and on and by walking up and down the stairs. One of the brothers had the shock of his life when an invisible entity turned the doorknob and opened the door. In addition, the disembodied voices of people talking have been heard downstairs. Although she has frightened more than one young man over the years, Ma seems to be a vigilant spirit that is just looking out for "her boys."

In an article in the *Murray State News* in October 28, 1988, Michael Powell wrote about treasurer James Thompson's encounter with the "friendly ghost" of the Delta Sigma Pi fraternity. Thompson stayed in the house with a fraternity brother, Lloyd Taylor, during Christmas break of 1980. They awoke one morning to find water running in the sink and the lights turned on in rooms that were unoccupied at the time. Their suspicions that they might be sharing the house with something otherworldly were confirmed a few nights later, when they returned home after dinner to find that the stereo and lights were on. The mischievous nature of the paranormal activity seemed to validate the rumor that the house was haunted by the ghost of a little boy whose father built the house. The story goes that the boy was playing around the roof when he fell to his death.

Another fraternity house on campus is that of Alpha Gamma Rho. According to Jennifer Potter, staff writer for the *Murray State News*, the house is haunted by the spirit of Elmus Jackson Beale. He is believed to have built the house in the 1930s. When he died, his funeral was held in the room that now serves as the fraternity's chapter room. Afterward, his body was carried through the window and buried in the yard. Since the fraternity moved into the house, the brothers' daily routines have been disrupted. Doors open on their own after they have been shut. Lights turn off and on. One of the fraternity members was upstairs all by himself when he heard someone running upstairs. He and two of his brothers searched the house for an intruder but found no one. Marvin Zwalen said that he has heard disembodied footsteps walk up to the door of his room and stop. No one ever enters. In 1993, a fraternity member named Stacy Williams was all alone in the house, watching television, when he heard somebody walk down the hall and stop in the doorway. He then heard a voice asking him how he was doing. Williams turned around and was surprised to see the figure of a man. After the strange man vanished, it occurred to Williams that he had probably had a visitation from the ghost of Elmus Beale. Scott McIntyre's encounter with Beale's spirit was even more terrifying. He said that he had been awakened but was unable to rise from his bed. He said it felt like someone was pinning him to the bed.

Not surprisingly, Murray State University also has the most common type of haunted building on college campuses: a haunted dormitory. The ghost haunting Hester Hall is the spirit of a young man who burned to death in Room 402. The building reopened the next year for freshmen only. One resident who lived in the room claimed to have felt something watching him when he was standing outside of the door. After a short while, the room was closed. Before long, students began spreading the rumor that the supposedly "locked" room was often found unlocked. Students who walked inside the room and shut the door swore that it opened on its own. In a variant of the legend, the young man was able to escape the fire after inhaling a great deal of smoke. He then staggered into the hallway and collapsed in front of Room 406. To this day, some students who have lived in Room 406 claimed to have heard a scratching sound on the door. When they opened it, no one was there.

Not every haunted building on the campus of Murray State University is a place where students live. Students say that the Fine Arts Building is haunted as well. Although the identity of the ghost that haunts the building is unknown, it is said to be the spirit of a female student who walked through the door of the elevator on the fourth floor, unaware that it was still on the first floor. She plummeted down the shaft and was killed instantly. Many students believe that her ghost is responsible for the rattling and shaking of the elevator as it goes up and down the shaft. It also stops on the fourth floor for no apparent reason. Students who ride the elevator have felt cold air wash over them.

Eastern Kentucky University (Richmond)

Eastern State Normal School No. 1 was founded in 1906 on the site of Central University, which had closed in 1901. In 1922, the institution changed its name to Eastern Kentucky State Normal School after becoming a four-year school. In 1928, the Southern Association of Colleges and Schools accredited the school. In 1930, it changed its name again, this time to Eastern Kentucky State Teachers College. Five years later, graduate courses were added to the curriculum. In 1948, the name of the institution was officially changed to Eastern Kentucky University. EKU's first doctorate degree was awarded in educational leadership and policy studies. Like many colleges and universities, EKU also offers online degrees.

Named after Kentucky's pioneering champion of public schools, Jere A. Sullivan, Sullivan Hall was built in 1912, supposedly on the site of a Civil War field hospital during the Battle of Richmond. Today, Sullivan Hall is believed to be haunted by the ghost of a nurse named Victoria who hanged herself in Room 425. The July 5, 2015 edition of the *Upward Branch Newsletter*

Several buildings on the campus of Eastern Kentucky University are believed to be haunted by the ghosts of a nurse and two students. *Courtesy of Wikimedia Commons.*

carried a story about the visit to the room by the writers, Taylor Lainhart and Whitney Ferrell. Their guide, a tutor advisor (TA) named Cheyenne Lewis, introduced the pair to other TAs who had had paranormal experiences in the dorm. The TAs told them that some of their personal belongings had been moved to a different location during the night. The TAs believed that the same entity was probably responsible for opening and closing doors and throwing a bottle of nail polish across the room. Room 325 is closed now, but students who have peered under the door swear that they saw a shadowy form swinging back and forth from the ceiling. Other students claim to have seen claw marks on the door.

The Buchanan Theatre in the Keen Johnson Building is home to EKU's best-known spirit, the Blue Lady. Luke Dodd, a professor in the biology department, said that the true identity of the Blue Lady is unknown. She appears in variants of the tale as either a heartbroken student or an actress who hanged herself in the theater. She manifests as a blue aura that encircles the clock tower.

Keene Hall is believed to be haunted as well. The ghost is the spirit of a young man who hanged himself on the sixteenth floor. For years, students and staff have heard strange noises in the night and seen doors open and close on their own. A resident assistant who stayed in Room 308 took a photograph of the ghost of an old man just before he flew through the ceiling to the room above.

WORKS CITED

Books

Abramson, Rudy. *Encyclopedia of Appalachia*. Knoxville: University of Tennessee Press, 2006.

Asher, Steve. *Hauntings of the Kentucky State Penitentiary*. Brentwood, TN: Permuted Press, 2016.

Bro, Harmon Hartzell. *Edgar Cayce: A Seer Out of Season*. London: Aquarian Press, 1990.

Brown, Alan. *Haunted Kentucky*. Mechanicsburg, PA: Stackpole, 2009.

Brown, Meredith Mason. *Frontiersman: Daniel Boone and the Making of America*. Baton Rouge: Louisiana State University, 2008.

Bush, Bryan, and Thomas Freese. *Haunted Battlefields of the South*. Atglen, PA: Schiffer Publishing, 2010.

Domine, David. *Phantoms of Old Louisville: Ghostly Tales from America's Most Haunted Neighborhood*. Kuttaway, KY: McClanahan Publishing House, 2006.

Draper, Lyman. *The Life of Daniel Boone*. Mechanicsburg, PA: Stackpole, 1998.

Ellis, William. *A History of Eastern Kentucky University: The School of Opportunity*. Bowling Green: University Press of Kentucky, 2001.

Faragher, John Mack. *Daniel Boone: The Life and Legend of an American Pioneer*. New York: Holt, 1992.

Hamilton, Mary. *Kentucky Folktales: Revealing Stories, Truths, and Outright Lies*. Lexington: University Press of Kentucky, 2012.

Henson, Michael Paul. *Tragedy at Devil's Hollow and Other Kentucky Ghost Stories*. Johnson City, TN: Overmountain Press, 1984.

Holland, Jeffrey Scott. *Weird Kentucky*. New York: Sterling Publishing, 2008.

Johnson, Larry. *The Seelbach: A Centennial Salute to Louisville's Grand Hotel*. Louisville, KY: Butler Books, 2004.

Kennedy, Frances. *The Civil War Battlefield Guide*. Boston: Houghton Mifflin Company, 1990.

Lofaro, Michael. *Daniel Boone: An American Life*. Lexington: University Press of Kentucky, 2012.

Montell, William Lynwood. *Ghosts across Kentucky*. Bowling Green: University Press of Kentucky, 2000.

———. *Haunted Houses and Family Ghosts of Kentucky*. Bowling Green: University Press of Kentucky, 2001.

Nickell, Joe. *The Mystery Chronicles: More Real-Life X-Files*. Bowling Green: University Press of Kentucky, 2004.

Simon, F. Kevin. *Federal Writers' Project of the Work Projects Administration for the State of Kentucky*. Lexington: University Press of Kentucky, 1996.

Steely, Michael S. *Swift's Silver Mines and Related Appalachian Treasures*. Johnson City, TN: Overmountain Press, 1995.

Windham, Kathryn Tucker. *Jeffrey Introduces 13 More Southern Ghosts*. Tuscaloosa: University of Alabama Press, 1971.

Woods, Ralph Hicks. *Fifty Years of Progress: A History of Murray State University*. Murray, KY: Murray State University, 1973.

Internet Articles

American Battlefield Trust. "John Hunt Morgan." www.battlefields.org.

American Hauntings. "The Legend of Octavia Hatcher: 'The Girl Who Turned Her Back on Pikesville.'" www.americanhauntingsink.com.

———. "Waverly Hills Sanatorium: Kentucky's Hospital of the Damned." www.americanhauntingsink.com.

America's Haunted Roadtrip. "The Ghosts of Perryville Battlefield." June 14, 2016. www.americashauntedroadtrip.com.

Amino Apps. "Camp Taylor: Seriously Haunted." March 29, 2019. https://aminoapps.com.

Amplifier. "The Mysteries of Octagon Hall: A Home to History and Hauntings." www.bgamplifier.com.

Anderson, Delonda. "The Devil in Appalachia—The Bloodthirsty Harpe Brothers." Appalachia Bare. October 17, 2019. www.appalachiabare.com.

Atlas Obscura. "The Corpse of a Cave Explorer That Became a Tourist Attraction." www.atlasobscura.com.

———. "Meet Spring-Heeled Jack, the Leaping Devil That Terrorized Victorian England." www.atlasobscura.com

———. "The Witches' Tree: Louisville, Kentucky." www.atlasobscura.com.

Barkerville. "Kentucky Cannibal in Cariboo: A Story of the Killer Boone Helm." http://www.barkerville.com.

Becky Linhardt. "General John Hunt Morgan—Hunt-Morgan House—Lexington." www.beckylinhardt.com.

Benedict, Adam. "Cryptid Profile: The Herrington Lake Eel-Pig." Pine Barren Institute. August 19, 2018. www.pinebarreninstitute.com.

———. "User Submitted Cryptid Sighting: Devil Monkey." Pine Barren Institute. September 4, 2018. www.pinebarrensinstitue.com.

Berk, Michael. "Lincoln County Man Claims to Have Found Swift's Mine." Lex18. January 31, 2020. www.lex18.com.

Bigthink. "Virgin Mary Apparitions: 17 Most Famous Appearances." https://bigthink.com.

Bit of the Bluegrass. "A Dark and Bloody Name." www.bitofthebluegrass.com.

———. "Ghosts of E.K.U." www.bitofthebluegrass.com.

Black Triangle. "The Sand Mountain Ghost Lights." August 1, 2010. www.theblacktriangle.blogspot.com.

Braden Investigations and Consulting. "Unsolved Homicide Florence, Ky." February 1, 2018. https://www.bradeninvestigations.com.

Brown Hotel. "A Brief History of a Long Louisville Tradition." https://www.brownhotel.com.

Brown Paper Tickets. "Bobby Mackey's Ghost Hunt: Bobby Mackey's Wilder, KY." www.brownpapertickets.com.

Burk, Tonja. "47 Years Later, Mountain Jane Doe Finally Has a Name." WBIR. September 22, 2016. https://www.wbir.com.

Cabral, Carrie. "Who Are the Blue People of Kentucky? Why Are They Blue?" Prep Scholar, November 2, 2019. https://blog.prepscholar.com.

Carey, Liz. "At Kentucky's Oldest Distilleries, Spirits Fill the Bourbon Barrels—and Haunt the Halls." Roadtrippers, October 20, 2019. https://roadtrippers.com.

Castner, Charles B. "A Brief History of the Louisville & Nashville Railroad." L&N. www.lnrr.org.

Cave Hill Cemetery Heritage Foundation. "Early History." https://www. cavehillcemetery.com.

Central Park Louisville. "History of Old Louisville's Central. www. oldlouisville.com.

Completely Kentucky. "Mantell UFO Incident." https://completely-kentucky.fandom.com.

———. "Paintsville UFO and Train Collision." https://completely-kentucky.fandom.com.

———. "Stanford Abduction." https://completely-kentucky.fandom.com.

———. "UFOs and the Government." https://completely-kentucky. fandom.com.

Crawford, Byron. "Mystery of Mandy." Kentucky Living. October 1, 2016. https://www.kentuckyliving.com.

Cryptid Wiki. "Pope Lick Monster." https://cryptidz.fandom.com.

Dave's Garden. "Kentucky Lake's Underwater Ghost Town." https:// davesgarden.com.

Day, Teresa. "Civil War Heritage." Visit Lex. July 6, 2020. https://www. visitlex.com.

Eigenheer, Michelle. "Let's All Drink with Ghosts in Louisville's Most Haunted Bars." Thrillist. October 17, 2016. https://www.thrillist.com.

Everson, Zach. "Meat Co-Founder to Open Meta Cocktail Bar Downtown this October." Louisville Eater. July 17, 2013. https://Louisville.eater.com.

Explore Kentucky Lake. "Land between the Lakes." https://www. explorekentuckylake.com.

Facebook.com. "Be Safe and Keep Your Powder Dry Written by Daryl Skaggs Is in Bardstown, Kentucky." www.facebook.com.

Fern Flower. "Mystical Tree Took the Form of a Murdered Woman." https://www.fern-flower.org.

Four Rivers Explorer. "Ghost Stories & the Paranormal of LBL." https:// www.fourriversexplorer.com.

———. "Vampire Hotel in Land between the Lakes." https://www. fourriversexplorer.com.

Fright Find. "The Brown Hotel." https://frightfind.com.

———. "Grandview Cemetery." www.frightfind.com.

Gee, Dawn. "Camp Taylor Neighborhood Sits on WWI Camp Site Where Many Died from Influenza." Derby City Weekend. https://www. derbycityweekend.com.

———. "Haunted Tales from the Louisville Palace." Derby City Weekend. derbycityweekend.com.

———. "Tales of KY's Gargoyle Like Creature Documented in Headlines." Wave 3 News, May 13, 2014. www.wave3.com.

Got Mountain Life. "Moon-Eyed People." May 25, 2018. https://gotmountainlife.com.

A Grave Interest. "The Haunted Brown Hotel—Louisville, Kentucky." October 10, 2020. https://agraveinterest.blogspot.com.

Harned, Carrie. "The Secret Life of the Seelbach Hotel." Wave 3 News. May 7, 2003. https://www.wave3.com.

Harris, Gardiner. "1993 Louisville Police Helicopter UFO." *Courier-Journal,* March 6, 1993. www.newspapers.com.

Haunted Attraction Online. "The Kentucky Meat Storm of 1876." http://hauntedattractiononline.com.

Haunted Houses. "Apparition of a Soldier from the War of 1812." www.hauntedhouses.com.

———. "The DuPont Mansion." www.hauntedhouses.com.

———. "The Hunt-Morgan House." www.hauntedhouses.com.

Haunted Places. "Lindsey Wilson College." hauntedplaces.org.

———. "Western Kentucky University." https://www.hauntedplaces.org.

Haunted Places of USA. "Union College, Pfeiffer Hall, Room 245, Barbourville, Kentucky." https://hauntedplacesofusa.blogspot.com.

Haunted Places to Go. "Castle on the Cumberland Considered One of the Most Haunted Places in Kentucky." https://www.haunted-places-to-go.com.

Haunted Rooms. "The Seelbach Hilton, Louisville." www.hauntedrooms.com.

Hayden, Joe. "A Guide to the Louisville Palace Theater and Its Rich History." Joe Hayden Realtor. October 13, 2013. www.joehaydenrealtor.com.

Historic Hotels of America. "The Seelbach Hilton, Louisville." www.historichotels.org.

History Collection. "18 Spooky Native American Monsters That Will Keep You Awake at Night." October 16, 2018. historycollection.com.

Horror History. "The Body of 'Tent Girl' Found." May 17, 2019. https://horrorhistory.net.

It's Something Wiki. "Devil Monkeys." https://itsmth.fandom.com.

James, Connor. "'Mountain Jane Doe' Buried Nearly 50 Years after Murder." WYMT. July 29, 2017. https://www.wymt.com.

James, Marcus. "America's Most Haunted Places: The Sexton House." Dread Central. dreadcentral.com.

James, Susan Donaldson. "Fugates of Kentucky: Skin Bluer than Lake Louise." ABC News. February 21, 2012. https://abcnews.go.com.

Janssen, Volker. "How the 'Little Green Men' Phenomenon Began on a Kentucky Farm." History. January 2, 2020. https://www.history.com.

Jeanette's Take on Life. "Mrs. Stella Cohen Peine, C.C. Cohen Restaurant, the Ghost." August 31, 2007. jeanettestakeonlife.blogspot.com.

Journal of the Bizarre. "Debunked: The Kentucky Meat Storm of 1876." May 3, 2015. http://www.bizarrejournal.com.

Kentucky Expeditions. "Kentucky Lost Treasure." https://kyexpeditions. webs.com.

Kentucky Haunted Houses. "Maple Hill Manor Bed and Breakfast—Springfield KY Haunted Place." www.kentuckyhauntedhouses.com.

Kentucky Historic Institutions. "Kentucky State Penitentiary: The Castle on the Cumberland. History." https:/kyhi.org.

Ky Forward. "JSH's KY: The Legends Are Legion That Ky's Soil Holds Secrets—of Treasures." http://www.kyforward.com.

Ky Kinfolk. "Hall's Half-Acre." www.kykinfolk.com.

Lakritz, Talia. "The Most Haunted Roads in the US and the Chilling Stories behind Them." Insider. September 28, 2020. https://insider.com.

Lasker, John. "Litle Green Men in the Bluegrass." Leo Weekly. October 26, 2011. https://leoweekly.com.

Legends of America. "Daniel Boone—The Kentucky Pioneer." www. legendsofamerica.com.

———. "The Vicious Harpes—First American Serial Killers." www. lengendsofamerica.com/we-harpes/

Lindsey.edu. "The History of LWC." lindsey.edu/about-lwc/History.cfm

Listverse.com. "10 Dark Facts about the Vampire Cult Killer Rod Ferrell."

Louisville Ghost Hunters Society. "The Legend of Sleepy Hollow." www. louisvilleghs.com.

———. "Louisville Ghost Hunters Explore Hot-Rod Hollow." www. louisvilleghs.com.

———. "The Palace Theatre." www.louisevilleghs.com.

Lovejoy, Bess. "10 Drowned Towns You Can Visit." Mental Floss. July 29, 2015. mentalfloss.com.

McCracken County Public Library. "Scary Places in Old Paducah: Hell's Half Acre, Pistol Avenue, Dogtown, Monkey Wrench Park, Hot Springs, and the Bucket of Blood." https://mclib.net/blogs.

McNamee, Gregory. "Daniel Boone: Myth and Reality." *Encyclopedia Britannica* (blog). October 23, 2007. blogs.britannica.com.

Marshall, Kelli. "4 People Who Were Buried Alive (And How They Got Out)." Mental Floss. February 15, 2014. https://www.mentalfloss.com.

Millard, Jamie. "Hauntings in Gratz Park." Smiley Pete Publishing. March 2, 2012. https://smileypete.com.

Monster Wiki. "Hellhound (Folklore)." www.monster.fandom.com.

Murderpedia. "Donald Harvey." www.murderpedia.org.

Museums of Historic Hopkinsville. "Edgar Cayce—The Early Years." www.mueseumsofhopkinsville.org.

My Old Kentucky Home. "History Overview." https://www.visitmyoldkyhome.com.

National Park Service. "Civil War Comes to the Cumberland Gap." www.nps.gov.

————. "Hunt-Morgan House." www.nps.gov.

National Parks Traveler. "Mammoth Cave National Park Harbors More than a Few Ghost Stories." October 30, 2009. www.nationalparktraveler.org.

National Register of Historic Places. "National Register of Historic Places Inventory—Nomination Form: Louisville Free Public Library." https://npgallery.nps.gov.

North Carolina Museum of History. "Daniel Boone Legacy." www.ncmuseumofhistory.org.

Only in Your State. "Bizarre Circumstances, History, and Mystery Combine at the Witches' Tree in Kentucky." www.onlyinyourstate.com.

————. "The Creepy Small Town in Kentucky with Insane Paranormal Activity." www.onlyinyourstate.com.

————. "Kasey Cemetery Is One of Kentucky's Spookiest Cemeteries." www.onlyinyourstate.com.

————. "The Kentucky Ghost Story That Will Leave You Absolutely Baffled." www.onlyinyourstate.com.

————. "Most People Have No Idea There's an Underwater Ghost Town Hiding in Kentucky." www.onlyinyourstate.com.

————. "Spend the Night at Kentucky's Most Haunted Campground for a Truly Terrifying Experience." www.onlyinyourstate.com.

Oxygen. "How 'The Vampire Clan' Went from Teen Blood Rituals to Killing Parents." https://www.oxygen.com.

Paranormal Milwaukee. "Octagon Hall Civil War Museum." https://paranormalmilwaukee.com.

The Parklands. "The Pope Lick Monster." September 29, 2011. www.theparklands.org.

Paulus, Caroline. "Buffalo Trace Gets a Visit from Ghost of Distilling Past." Bourbon Review. August 6, 2017. https://www.gobourbon.com.

People of the Hunting Ground. "The Yahoo Falls Massacre." www.thepeopleofthehuntingground.com.

Pirtle, Caleb, and Linda. "What Are Those Mysterious UFOs Doing above Kentucky?" Caleb and Linda Pirtle. March 9, 2019. https://calebandlindapirtle.com.

Pisterman, Lisa. "Who Is the Real 'Lady in Blue' of Seelbach Hotel?." Leo Weekly, October 24, 2018. https://www.leoweekly.com.

Powell, Lewis. "Spirits of Old Morrison and the Gratz Park Historic District." Southern Spirit Guide, October 11, 2010. www.southernspiritguide.org.

———. "Van Meter Hall." Southern Spirit Guide. www.southernspiritguide.org.

Prickett, Kathy. "The Terrifying Story of the 'Hell Hound.'" BBC News, October 31, 2015. www.bbc.com.

The Real Waverly Hills. "Waverly Hills Sanatorium." www.therealwaverlyhills.com.

Richkoff, Cheryl Adams. "Facts About the Kentucky Cannibal That'll Keep You Up at Night." Ranker. April 21, 2020. https://www.ranker.com.

Roadside America. "Jesse James' Pane of Glass." www.roadsideamerica.com.

———. "LaGrange, Kentucky: LaGrange Host Tour: Jennie the Typhoid Girl." www.roadsideamerica.com.

———. "Lightning Portrait of Startled Lady Bather." www.roadsideamerica.com.

Schulz, G.W. "Kentucky Authorities Identify Mountain Jane Doe.'" Muck Rack. www.muckrack.com.

Smith, A. "Rebel Rock: The Story of Harlan County, Kentucky's Civil War Legend and the KKK." Medium. June 30, 2015. https://medium.com.

Southern Spirit Guide. "'The Groaning of the Prisoner'—Kentucky State Penitentiary." November 27, 2019. www.southernspiritguide.org.

Spencer, Dave. "Hancock County Can Claim Most Recent Kentucky Bigfoot Sighting." WBKR. November 21, 2019. https://wbkr.com.

Still They Speak. "Unsolved Homicide: Otha Young, Jr." www.stilltheyspeak.com.

Survey Monkey. "The Moon-Eyed People." www.surveymonkey.com.

Tennessee State Library and Archives. "Daniel Boone." https://sharetngov.tnsosfiles.com/tsla.

Theresa's Haunted History of the Tri-State. "Debunking a Cemetery Legend." March 10, 2014. https://theresashauntedhistoryofthetri-state.blogspot.com

———. "The Hell Hound of Baker Hollow Road Cemetery." October 15, 2014. https://theresashauntedhistoryofthetri-state.blogspot.com

———. "Lexington's Haunted Gratz Park Inn." June 28, 2014. https://thereashauntedhistoryofthetri-state.blogspot.com.

30 Days of Kentucky Archaeology. "The Myth of Kentucky as a 'Dark and Bloody Ground.'" September 29, 2017. https://30daysofkentuckyarchaeology.wordpress.com.

Today I Found Out. "The Mystery of the Kentucky Meat Shower." July 27, 2015. http://www.todayifoundout.com.

Todd, Whitney. "Union College." Explore Kentucky History. https://explorekyhistory.ky.gov.

Travel Channel. "Bobby Mackey's Haunted History." www.travelchannel.com.

Tumblr. "Wanna See Something Weird?" cryptids-of-the-world-tumblr.com.

University of Kentucky Press. "The Truth Is Out There: An Excerpt from REAL-LIFE X-FILES." https://kentuckypress.wordpress.com.

Unsolved Mysteries Wiki. "Nancy Daddysman." https://unsolvedmysteries.fandom.com/wiki.

Unusual Kentucky. "The Haunted Restrooms of EKU." June 30, 2008. www.unusualkentucky.blogspot.com.

———. "UFO Blitz in the Bluegrass Triangle." March 30, 2011. www.unusualkentucky.blogspot.com.

Utley, Harold. "The Story of the Harp Brothers." Webster County. www.webstercoky.com.

Visit Hopkinsville. "17 Reasons to Love Hopkinsville. Edgar Cayce." https://www.visithopkinsville.com.

WDRB.com. "After Long Wait, Louisville's 'Hot Rod Haven' Will Be Fixed." May 24, 2020. wdrb.com.

Western Kentucky University. "History and Traditions." https://www.wku.edu.

Western KY History. "The Sleeping Prophet: Edgar Cayce, 1877–1945." westernkyhistory.org.

WNC Magazine. "The Real Daniel Boone: Legends Paint a Larger-than-Life Picture of the Woodsman, but at Heart He Was a Simple Man Driven By Curiosity." September 2010. https://wncmagazine.com.

WPSD. "Remembering an Underewater Town in Marshall County, Kentucky." October 31, 2015. www.psdlocal6com.

———. "Stories of the Castle on the Cumberland." October 31, 2017. https://www.wpsdlocal6.com.

The Wytchery. "Urban Legends: Mysteries as Dark as the Night from a Sleepy Hollow Road in Kentucky." https://www.gothichorrorstories.com.

Magazines/Journals

Allen, James Lane. "Through the Cumberland on Horseback." *Harper's Magazine*, 1886.

Molck, Katie. "Legend of the Witches' Tree." *Louisville Magazine*, October 26, 2015.

Owen, Brent. Spirited Tales." *Kentucky Monthly*, October 1, 2017.

Windsor, Pam. "Ghost Soldiers." *Kentucky Living*, October 10, 2014.

Witthoft, John, and Wendell S. Haddock. "Cherokee-Iroquois Little People." *Journal of American Folklore* 59, no. 234 (October–December 1946): 413+.

Newspapers

Austin, Emma. "GHOST MAP: We Dare You to Explore These 300+ Haunted Places in Kentucky and Indiana." *Louisville Courier-Journal*, October 19, 2020.

Cincinnati Enquirer. "Sepulcher Containing the Skeletons of Prehistoric Giants Is Unearthed in Kentucky." November 24, 1911.

Cole, Heather. "Haunted Halls of Union College." *Times Tribune* (Corbin, KY), October 31, 2007.

Farris, David. "The Cherokee Legend of the Little People." *Edmond (OK) Life & Leisure*, January 29, 2015.

Ghabour, Dahlia. "Pizza with a Side of Ghosts? Inside Some of Louisville's Most Haunted Bars and Restaurants." *Louisville Courier-Journal*, October 27, 2020.

Harlan Enterprise. "Mountain Jane Doe Documentary to Screen." March 21, 2018. Horne, Sarah. "After 40 Years, Bobby Mackey's 'Come for the Ghosts, Stay for the Music' Keeps Going." *Cincinnati Enquirer*, January 3, 2019,

Kentucky Standard. "Notorious Brothers Frank and Jesse James Had Family Connection to Chaplin." September 13, 2011.

Kuhl, Sara. "MADSOCIAL: Eku's Ghost Stories—Dodd Talks Supposed Hauntings on Campus." *Richmond (KY) Register*, October 27, 2018.

Lainhart, Taylor, and Whitney Ferrell. "Haunting of Sullivan Hall." *Upward Branch*, July 5, 2012.

Operle, Derek. "Some Say Ghost Haunts C.C. Cohen Building." *Paducah (KY) Sun*, October 31, 2019.

Potter, Jennifer. "Ghost Haunts Alpha Gamma Rho Fraternity House." *Murray (KY) State News*, October 26, 1995.

Powell, Michael. "Halloween Resurrects Old Stories of Spooks." *Murray State News*, October 28, 1988.

Speakman, Burton. "Sheriff Focused on 1998 Murder." *Bowling Green (KY) Daily News*, January 6, 2007.

Owingsville (KY) Outlook. "The Sprinkle Dollar." March 24, 1898.

Story, Justin. "WKU's Haunted Halls." *Bowling Green Daily News*, October 24, 2007.

Taylor, Dave. "Researchers: Bigfoot Is Here." *Hancock (KY) Clarion*, November 9, 2017.

Theiss, Nancy Sterarns. "Liberty Hall and Blue Wing: The Brown Family Legacy, Part I." *Louisville Courier Journal*, October 3, 2017.

Warren, Beth. "Pope Lick 'Monster' Survivor Mentally Crushed." *Louisville Courier-Journal*, May 6, 2016.

Webb, Joh. "An EPD Officer Saw Strange Lights over the City. No One Knows What They Were." *Evansville Courier & Press*, February 3, 2021.

ABOUT THE AUTHOR

Dr. Alan Brown is an award-winning professor of English at the University of West Alabama. He has a deep interest in southern folklore, especially southern ghostlore and African American culture and music, and he has written over thirty books. When Dr. Brown is not teaching or writing, he enjoys reading thrillers and watching movies. He also does a little ghost hunting on the side. His favorite activities, however, include traveling to haunted places with his wife, Marilyn, and playing with his two grandsons, Cade and Owen.

CPSIA information can be obtained
at www.ICGtesting.com
Printed in the USA
BVHW091134251021
619817BV00002B/95